god.online

Seeking God
in the
21st Century

James C. Wetherbe, Ph.D.

Mead Publishing ❖ Houston, Texas

god.online

Seeking God
in the
21ˢᵗ Century

Copyright © 2003, MEAD PUBLISHING

PRINTED AND BOUND BY WORZALLA
STEVENS POINT, WISCONSIN USA

Published by Mead Publishing
P.O. Box 680324
Houston, TX 77268-0324

ISBN 1-883096-03-0

Mead Publishing books are available at special discounts for bulk purchases by corporations, institutions, and other organizations.

For more information, please contact Mead Publishing at:

Email: meadpublishing@houston.rr.com

or visit our Web site: http://www.godonlinebook.com

To family and friends

Table of Contents

Table of Contents
Continued

PREFACE

I am an unlikely person to write a book about God. It's the only spiritual book I've ever authored. Previously, I authored or co-authored 20 books mostly in the field of Management and Information Technology. As a rule I don't enjoy writing books, I enjoy having written books. It's the finished product that's gratifying.

I have no special training in religious study or even philosophy. My only qualifications:

❖ The issue of God and his existence has been a major life pursuit.

❖ My *nerd* training as a university researcher; disciplined, logical thinking after years of writing computer software.

❖ My strong motivation to find God combined with my research and logic training provide a different approach to seeking God. Empirical research methods and logical thinking allows readers to investigate the existence of God by relying on what they can personally experience and reason.

This book was an endeavor of love written with a passion I never experienced in authoring any other. It is the result of a lifetime of struggling to believe God really exists. The Bible says many times, if we seek we will find; I labored at faith. And failed often. Because of my skeptical nature, true faith didn't come easily; religious, ritual faith didn't satisfy me. At the same time, I really wanted to believe God existed and that I could be connected, *online* with Him.

In the end, I learned that faith is a gift – wonderful, fragile – and when operational offers a peaceful mind and meaning to life.

I promised God if He convincingly revealed Himself to me, I would dedicate myself to serving Him. For reasons that are clear to me now, He didn't give me instant gratification on my faith request. Rather He first allowed me worldly success. Why? Just to make sure I knew that it would not fulfill me – bring me happiness. Not only was worldly success not enough, it brought me troubles I could have never imagined.

Instead, I needed true spiritual success.

But God did reveal Himself to me in convincing ways, so I am keeping my promise to Him, and this book is part of that effort.

As my amazing wife of 34 years witnessed, I have never been more devoted or intense while writing a book. She lost much sleep because of my writing spells during the nights.

I've never worked harder as an author or accomplished so much in so little time, and I grew spiritually as a result of writing this book. When applying the authoring disciplines required in developing text, issues I thought resolved proved not to be. Through those struggles I not only gained clarity, I also gained a closer connection to God.

If you are a skeptic or are trying to help someone who is, this book is my gift to you.

ACKNOWLEDGEMENTS

An author never does it alone. First I want to thank my wife Smoky for thoroughly yet gently reviewing the first draft of each chapter. She is a wonderful wife and mother. Though she earned a Ph.D. from the University of Minnesota, she generously and effectively became the "at home" parent for our daughters so I could travel the world in pursuit of my career as professor and author.

My daughter Jamie who is both a poet and a journalist labored over my rough manuscript to make it read far beyond my authoring ability. My younger daughter Jessie is an author and a psychologist. She helped critique my attempts to make behavioral research more understandable. My brother Bond, who previously co-authored a book with me, also edited the book along with his wife Faye, an English major, entrepreneur and writer. Bond's logical/analytical thinking caught holes in my reasoning. Working on the book provided a wonderful opportunity for our family to have many candid, frank discussions about God and our faith that helped us all grow spiritually.

After my family provided the first reality check to see if what was in my head was responsibly getting to text, I had the benefit of having numerous wonderful colleagues and friends comb through the text and make many helpful suggestions. The goal was to make the book intellectually rigorous, yet readily accessible, a challenge to atheists and agnostics, and reassuring or at least not offensive to those of faith. It took quite a portfolio of reviewers to achieve all perspectives. I want to thank each of them for their patience and guidance.

Special thanks to Brad Anderson, Dr. Glenn Browne, Bob and Cathy Buday, Harry Burkstaller, John and Martha Childs, Dr. Gordon Davis, Wayne and Jane Farrell, Jim Glover, Richard and Vickie Grebe, Jared Hayman, Jim Holder, Dr. Brian Janz, Brynn Jones, Donnie and Kim Loerwald, Tom and Diane Lucas, Rob Mahon, Charles Orr, Joe Scofield, Donna Slayback, Bob Tero, Mark Thompson, Dr. Nicholas and Martha Vitalari, Dr. John Vawter, Jim Zanios and Dr. Bob Zimmer.

ABOUT THE AUTHOR

Dr. James C. Wetherbe is a highly regarded professor, author, and consultant of management and technology. He has spent more than 30 years in academia and industry, serving on the faculty at the University of Houston, University of Minnesota and the University of Memphis. Since May 2000, he has been the Stevenson Chair of Information Technology at Texas Tech University where he originally received his Ph.D. in 1976. He has lectured and consulted worldwide on management and information technology.

In this book, God's existence is explored in a straightforward and compelling way using empirical research and logical reasoning. Dr. Wetherbe has always been appreciated for his ability to explain complex computer technology to executives, managers and students. He applies those skills to explain how and why believing in God is logical, reasonable, and rewarding.

Prior to this book he authored or co-authored 20 books in his professional field. He was the first recipient of the *Management Information Systems Quarterly* Distinguished Scholar Award and was ranked as one of the top consultants in his field by *Information Week*. His book about FedEx, *The World on Time* (Knowledge Exchange 1995), was ranked in 1997 by Executive Book Summaries as one of the top 30 business books from more than 1,500 written. *Computing Newsletter* ranked his book *Systems Analysis and Design* (West 1979, 1984, 1988, 1994) as the best textbook on the topic. Other books include *Information Technology for Management* (Wiley 1996, 1999, 2002, 2004), *Computer Information Systems for Management* (West 1988), *Executive's Guide to Computer-Based Information Systems* (Prentice Hall 1983*), The Management of Information Systems* (McGraw Hill 1985), and *So, What's Your Point* (Mead Publishing 1993, 1998, 2003).

CHAPTER 1

INTRODUCTION

What is life's meaning? Is there a God? Is there life after death? How can I have peace and contentment? These are questions that have perplexed and even haunted me most of my life. If they are challenging to you or people you care about and you have a couple of hours, I hope this book will be helpful. It is the purpose for which it was written. In particular, you will find this book aimed at the *strong-willed* and spiritually *challenged* person who needs convincing, intellectual proof of God.

George Harrison of the Beatles died the day I was completing this introduction. His wife said that George had concluded that the search for God was the most important task in life. I agree.

God blessed me with worldly success far beyond my expectations. Though I spent considerable time in high-tech business, most of my career has been spent as a professor of information technology and management. Nonetheless, through book royalties, consulting and speaking honorariums, I surprisingly became an affluent professor (an oxymoron). But I always struggled for the greater meaning of things – to understand and believe in God. I became highly motivated to resolve this issue as a result of my closest friend Jim Evans dying when we were *only* 18: It should have been an immortal age. Death was for grandparents and seemed so far away as to be irrelevant. Suddenly reality changed: Death became proximate instead of distant.

After Jim died, I spent much of my life worrying about dying and what it meant. I wanted to believe in God and heaven. I'd been brought up in church and educated in the Christian faith, but as years passed I became *faith* deficient. Becoming a professor didn't help.

Academicians are by nature a skeptical lot, which is why so many are agnostics and atheists. The scientific approaches used by academicians to systematically derive knowledge from observation, study and experimentation demand high standards before conclusions are drawn. That training made me even more skeptical. Applying a scholarly standard to something as abstract and invisible as God made faith a major challenge.

To make matters worse, I spent much of my early career as a computer programmer. To successfully write software, your logic must be impeccably precise: One little logic flaw and the software won't perform correctly. The discipline of writing software developed a strong competency for ensuring my logic was solid. That was great for being a programmer and later helped me as an author, but disciplined, logical thinking made it difficult for me to believe. Reasoning combined with the *God evidence* I observed was not sufficiently convincing.

Both of my parents were Christians of strong faith and devoted students of the Bible. That faith served them well, especially later in their lives as they each faced their respective deaths. It was comforting to see the peace their faith brought them as they were dying. I wasn't sure that their faith was based on reality, but it was comforting to them and therefore comforting to me. I regretted that I couldn't just believe as they did, but my analytical, nature would not allow it, regardless of my desire.

When I discussed faith issues with my parents and others of any faith, I found holes in their logic. I became so proficient at challenging people's faith that *I quit doing it.* Finding logic flaws in people's belief systems was hurtful because I would often bewilder them or weaken their faith, and it wasn't helping my own. Superficial or new believers were especially vulnerable. I thought to myself, if there is a God and a devil, the devil might be using me in a dangerous way. I finally decided to tell people "good for you" if you've got faith, but please don't try to convince me. You won't help me, and conversation in this area with me could be *hazardous* to your faith.

WORLDLY SUCCESS VS. SPIRITUAL SUCCESS

Ironically, I think much of my worldly success resulted from my keeping myself so work-focused that I had less time to consider the really *important stuff* of life – not that I didn't try. Intensity and passion are in my character. In my early 30s I realized that I wasn't making much progress, and *important stuff* became increasingly troubling because I now had two wonderful daughters, Jamie and Jessie. I felt responsible for guiding them in their spiritual development, and I was ill-equipped. I also desired spiritual growth in my marriage to my wife Smoky.

Accordingly I engaged my most intense effort ever to resolve the God issue. I spent a year reading the Bible cover to cover using study guides. I even went to Jerusalem – *corporate headquarters* for the Jewish, Islamic and Christian religions. I invited my pastor at the time, Dr. John Vawter, to join me with the understanding I could ask any skeptical question and get a straight answer. John is no *pushover*, so we had some engaging conversations.

The result of my efforts was surprisingly quite positive. My belief increased, and I felt connected – *online* with God. I remember calling Jim Evan's mother, Ruth, to share my progress. A woman of incredible faith, she was delighted. But she quickly warned me that I would be more vulnerable than ever to *spiritual warfare* – good and evil. I likely would be subjected to faith challenging thoughts and events. She was right. Within months I was a *Doubting Thomas* again, but more about that later.

You may have guessed that by virtue of writing this book I have finally sorted out my issues concerning God's existence. I am at *peace* with it at last. Nonetheless, I am still *peace* in progress. Much about God and the Bible are still a mystery to me. But my doubts about His existence are gone.

As an academician I attempt to conduct and report research as objectively as possible. However in fairness to you as a reader, I should disclose a possible bias since I am now a Christian: I believe in God and attempt to follow the example and teachings of Christ. I have deliberately tried to keep that bias out of the logic in my argument of God's existence. This book is merely an attempt to share my painful, frustrating and lengthy spiritual journey in hopes it might make yours less problematic. By reading this book you will see what a skeptical nature I have and how that actually provides credibility to the process I used to achieve/receive faith.

This book is written for both skeptics *and* for those of faith who wish to help skeptics. As a courtesy and convenience for those who believe in God, this book includes Bible references periodically to reinforce that certain statements are indeed Biblical. For other readers who are in any way encouraged by the book, you might find reading the references helpful.

Returning to my visit to the Holy Land, when the Israelites left Egypt they wandered in the desert 40 years before coming to the Promised Land. When I went to Israel, I had the opportunity to see the Promised Land and its distance from Egypt. It should have taken eleven days to make the walk had the Israelites not lengthened their painful, frustrating journey through their faith deficiencies. Because of my faith deficiencies, I spent 40 years of my life trying to understand and get a tight connection to God. I promised God if I could ever achieve/receive faith that with His help I would spend the rest of my life helping others by sharing what He revealed to me.

This book is part of that commitment. I also promised God that since He had already blessed me financially, I would never take a penny for the time I used to serve Him. My skeptical nature makes me cautious of anyone asking for money for any reason. So for credibility and spirituality purposes of this book, I receive no author royalties. They are donated to other ministries and worthy causes.

INFORMATION OVERLOAD IN THE 21st CENTURY

As an educator in the information technology field. I often find that sophisticated technologists have a harder time achieving faith – especially when reading material from the Bible authored thousands of years ago by 'low-tech' prophets and apostles in sandals.

Nevertheless, one can quickly discover Biblical characters spent a great deal of time pondering and debating the reality of God and life's meaning. They had to toil at manual labor for food, i.e., mostly farming, and the other basic necessities and most of their work did not involve high mental energy as required in the knowledge economy of today. Also there were no TVs, DVDs, CDs, radios or video games to entertain/distract them – even written literature was limited.

Consequently they had more time to spend thinking, conversing and praying. I believe this is reflected in the longevity their recorded cognitive processes, i.e., the Bible, have attained. Though their work skills are archaic by current standards, God's message written through them is not.

Hard to Just Keep Up

I often fear that in our high-tech world we are so busy keeping up with the latest technology and the resulting information overload that we spend far too little time contemplating spiritual issues. We may be sophisticated from a technical perspective but risk being uneducated and shallow from a spiritual perspective.

An opening line I often use in my technology speeches is, "How many of you are overwhelmed by the increasing number of things you know less and less about?" It always results in a nervous round of laughter. I follow that question with, "How many of you are just hoping you can make it to retirement before you are obsolete?" More nervous laughter.

Air travel frequently exposes my *obsolescence* as I invariably sit next to someone who asks me what I do for a living. When I tell them I am a professor of information technology, they often get excited thinking they can now get answers to all of their 'tech' questions. They might say something like, "I'm having trouble logging on to the Internet with my daughter's computer, what am I doing wrong?" If I respond, "I really don't know," they usually look disappointed and skeptically ask, "Where do you teach?" Rather than tell them what I really do, I'm tempted to tell them that I am a proctologist – halting any further inquiries into my work.

Treadmill of Technology

At any rate, there's a serious downside to our high-tech world because we have more mental demands and distractions than ever before. It can be overwhelming to keep up with the knowledge needed just to survive in the secular/non-spiritual world. Making time to consider spiritual issues can be a challenge. Because technology is changing at such a rapid rate, I know that much of what I write in the area of technology soon becomes obsolete. Yet wisdom available from the Bible authored thousands of years ago, still remains profoundly relevant.

At the peak of my professional career I was giving more than 150 speeches annually all over the world, averaging a new book each year, advising Ph.D. students and concurrently directing two research centers at two different universities. I was so busy chasing my *secular* work that *spiritual* issues dropped off my radar screen. **But God Knows How to Get on Your Calendar.**

Dr. Phil McGraw is a popular psychologist and author of *Self Matters* (Simon Schuster, 2001) and has come to be affectionately known as Dr. Phil through his affiliation with the *Oprah Winfrey Show*. He made a profound statement about God during a broadcast of *Oprah*: "Often God will gently nudge you trying to get your attention. If that doesn't work he will eventually drop a piano on you."

I got the *grand* piano treatment – more than once. Through those experiences, God *freed* some time on my booked calendar for me to seriously pray and think. And I did, thank God. During one of those times, I discovered a useful metaphor to help comprehend God.

21st CENTURY METAPHOR FOR COMPREHENDING GOD

Trying to comprehend something as abstract and invisible as God is a challenge. As educators we often use analogies or metaphors to explain the complicated or hard to understand. In this way we can use something that our students are *familiar* with to help them comprehend something that is *unfamiliar*. Jesus, who even atheists generally regard as a great *moral* teacher, often used this technique through the *parable* format. For example, Jesus used the wind as a metaphor to help explain the Holy Spirit, e.g., John 3:8.

Within my field of expertise I found an excellent 21st Century metaphor that has proven useful to help people understand our relationship to God – the *Internet*. Specifically, I refer to the *wireless* use of *the Net*.

The concept of God as an invisible spirit that can be everywhere and available to anyone via prayer was always mind-boggling for me – even more so when realizing the *invisible* concept was first written about thousands of years ago.

Conceptually similar are the radio, television, wireless telephone and Internet waves surrounding you wherever you're reading this book – you just can't see them. Though invisible, you know they are there: All you have to do is turn on a radio, television, cell phone or wireless Internet device to access them.

The wireless Internet device is the best metaphor – a computing device that has powerful stand-alone capabilities – just as a person does. By connecting to the Internet, the previously stand-alone device *exponentially* increases in functionality. The Internet offers global access to amazing knowledge/processing capacity and is concurrently available to any device capable of going *online*. It is also capable of tracking or *profiling* our behavior, including what information we routinely access as well as our shopping patterns.

These aspects of the Internet make it a good metaphor for an all-knowing, omnipresent God. The emergence of the *human-created* Internet makes comprehending God's amazing abilities less of an *intellectual stretch*.

An important step is required to go *online* regardless of where you are in the world: You must decide to do so. You can do that by clicking the 'Yes' option on your computer, or by programming it to go *online* automatically when you flip the 'On' switch. Similarly, I have found that to access God (invisible as He is) you have to make a conscious, prayerful decision to go *online* with Him in order to access the amazing wisdom and guidance He provides.

God tells us throughout the Bible that if we earnestly seek, we will find Him, e.g., Jeremiah 29:13, 1 Chronicles 28:9, Psalms 119:2, Proverbs 8:17, Matthew 7:7, Luke 12:31, Romans 2:7 and Hebrews 11:16. This promise from God is key to the approach to proof presented in this book: We must *seek* God to go *online* with Him.

Just as *computer viruses* and *worms* created by *hackers* are negative Internet elements, which against our wishes can destroy our information and ability to process correctly, in this metaphor, viruses and worms are satanic forces, e.g., 2 Corinthians 11:14. Viruses – like evil – are often deceptively disguised, pretending to be friendly email messages or greeting cards from a friend or another well-intended person. That's how they *dupe* the unsuspecting into opening them and then inflict their destructive consequences. On the other hand, computer worms that promulgate from computer to computer via networks without human intervention, i.e., sending an email, are *blatantly* evil. Although we want to take advantage of all the Internet has to offer, we need to guard ourselves against computer viruses and worms. Similarly though we want to be open to God, we need to guard ourselves against evil.

Though educational, metaphors *don't* prove anything – including God's existence. Providing proof is the goal of the remainder of the book.

CONCLUSION

Please don't think that I believe I've cornered the market on proof of God's existence. There have been wonderful, helpful books that explain the Bible and/or give compelling reasons to have faith in God. The way I found God is just one of many means. God reveals Himself in many diverse ways to those who seek Him.

Previous Works

Authored by C.S. Lewis during World War II and published shortly thereafter, *Mere Christianity* (Harper, 1952) is a terrific book for seekers. Lewis used incredibly straightforward and insightful reasoning to argue for the existence of God. To a great extent, I have tried to build on C. S. Lewis' work by providing a 21st century context.

Besides *Mere Christianity*, there is considerable literature using evidentiary, journalistic, philosophical, physical science, archaeological, and aesthetic evidence (design and beauty of nature arguments) for God's existence. Unfortunately in spite of my efforts with this material, I remained skeptical. I struggled with a few logic issues in Lewis' work. Evidentiary approaches, i.e., judging evidence as if presented in a court of law, though compelling, were suspect to me. The number of criminals all of us have seen *getting away with murder* has dampened my trust of evidentiary approaches for achieving faith. And journalistic approaches, though insightful, were problematic for me because I've been misquoted occasionally and am familiar with enough incidents of inaccurate reporting to make me cautious of that approach. Archaeological arguments help many people, but facts based upon carbon dating never quite did it for me. Aesthetic evidence deserves it's own discussion, treated later in the book. While some of my good Christian friends found faith in God through these evidences, I've also learned that God is not limited to revealing Himself to us in any particular way.

If I Seek, Will I Find?

After years of frustration I just started praying to God, "If you exist, please reveal yourself to me. I want to believe, but my mind is unwilling, and I am struggling. Please help." The prayer wasn't immediately answered. Gratefully, over time, learning to apply empirical research methods, logic and faith, I finally got *online* with God.

Building a Bridge of Faith

If you will, imagine achieving faith as building a bridge that takes us from a place of *non-believing* across a canyon to a place of *believing*. We build that 'faith' bridge with *information*. If we don't have faith, it's because we have insufficient information, or we are ignoring the information available to us. I was a victim of the first and guilty of the latter. And God is not done with me yet.

If you haven't already done so, I truly hope the information provided in this book will help you build your bridge. If not, please don't despair. Information that builds a bridge for one person may not provide the perspective or insights needed for another. Many people have successfully built their bridge from existing literature, but in my case, this just couldn't get the job done. God helped me build my bridge – patiently, but due to my stubbornness, not always gently. This book documents the information He provided me; if it doesn't help you, look elsewhere and pray. Whatever you do, please just keep seeking.

Organization of the Book

The remainder of the book shares the proof and processes that showed me the way. **Chapter 2** discusses why faith can be so difficult – especially for the skeptic. **Chapter 3** provides some ground rules on how we as humans can *know-what-we-know* using empirical science and logic. **Chapter 4** explores ways to *know-what-we-don't-know*, including arriving at surprisingly positive ways to understand more about death. **Chapter 5** provides a way for you to find empirical and logical evidence of God's existence. In **Chapter 6**, I share some *epiphanies* God has provided through prayer to answer some of my deepest, most troubling God issues. Let's begin **Chapter 2** and explore reasons why faith can be difficult for the skeptical.

CHAPTER 2

WHY WE STRUGGLE WITH FAITH
AND
UNDERSTANDING GOD

There are several reasons why we struggle with faith and understanding God. The first reason is our initial faith, whatever it might be, is typically a result of what we are (or not) taught as a child – usually by our parents. The faith of a child tends to be a blind, unchallenged faith. It is a faith that comes easy. Most children in Western culture are convinced to believe in Santa Claus, the Tooth Fairy and the Easter Bunny.

They find out sometime in early childhood that the *trinity* of Santa Claus, the Easter Bunny and the Tooth Fairy is totally bogus. This revelation is usually a result of *older, wiser* children telling them – to the dismay of the newly informed children and their respective parents. Or sometimes as children grow older and their reasoning skills develop, they just start *questioning* the validity of this *childhood trinity*. Even a little childhood logical analysis reveals to most children the logistical challenges of Santa Claus getting to every house in the world in one night; his ability to be at every shopping mall is also clearly suspect. And of course there is the whole issue of Santa Claus getting his full-figure physique down the chimney. It takes even less childhood reasoning to eliminate the Easter Bunny and the Tooth Fairy as viable characters.

Less analytical children often discover the reality of these childhood beliefs because their parents *slip* up. For example children wake up too early and catch Santa in the act, Mom or Dad might be seen filling the Easter basket, or the Tooth Fairy might forget.

When children effectively challenge any member of the childhood trinity based upon their logic and/or observations, parents have to *fess up*. For example, one day when my daughter Jamie was seven years old she simply asked her mother, "Mom are you the Tooth Fairy?" My wife replied, "Jamie, I always told myself that when you asked I would tell you the truth," and she did. Jamie then asked, "Are you the Easter Bunny and Santa Claus too?" My wife *gulped* and confessed the whole hoax.

In one *fell-swoop* the childhood trinity went down. Jamie, as other children do, had begun to question her *reality*. My wife had Jamie make a vow of secrecy. She was not to reveal to her younger sister the discovery she had made by the 'ruthless' interrogation of her mother. Jamie honored that vow, but it didn't matter. Jessie figured it out soon enough. Initially my wife and I thought she had obtained the information *illegally* from her older cousins. But she had figured it out on her own using her reasoning skills. She verified her hypothesis with her Mom for whom acknowledging the hoax was easier the second time around. Fortunately for me, I was out of town for both occasions keeping me off of the 'verification hook.' Christmas, Easter and the loss of a tooth were never quite the same – appropriately so. We can't be children forever.

As children discover the truth about the childhood trinity, they usually don't consider this to be serious fraudulent behavior on the part of the parents they trusted. Rather they tend to see it as a *ritual* of childhood. They have *graduated*, if you will, and are now too wise to believe such nonsense. In fact most children are proud of their newly found wisdom. So much so it is difficult for them to resist the temptation (in spite of *lethal* threats from parents) to enlighten the naive *fools* who still believe.

HAVE I BEEN FOOLED ABOUT GOD TOO?

As a child I believed in God because my parents believed. Most children do, in my experience, whether they are brought up Muslim, Jewish, Christian or any other faith. For some people their faith is never questioned or really challenged. However, for many their faith gets challenged and examined, as they become adults. For me it was when I went off to college.

As I mentioned in **Chapter 1**, agnostics and atheists are commonplace on university campuses; they can really work you over. Questions like, "How do you really know there is a God?" or "Don't you realize your religious beliefs are based upon what your parents told you to believe?" (The really vicious ones would even bring up the whole childhood trinity business and stick it to you.) Realizing you would likely believe any religion you were taught as a child can quickly challenge a child-based, superficial faith – a phenomenon common in universities regardless of generation.

Thirty years after I went off to college, my nephew Scott attended a youth ministry meeting and was clobbered by a question that others often stumble over. One of the Bible discussion leaders explained the Christian faith including accepting Jesus Christ as your Savior. Scott asked, "How does that work for someone, say in a remote tropical jungle, who has never even heard of Jesus Christ?" The leader, apparently not aware of how that issue is addressed in the Bible, incorrectly instructed that those people were unfortunately not *saved.* (**Chapter 5** addresses this issue – but that's for later.)

Scott told the leader that he wasn't interested in a God that was that unfair. He left the meeting and never went back. I heard Scott's story, and it made me sad. It reminded me of some of my college *faith-shaking* experiences.

Sometime later I offered Scott the first draft of **Chapter 1** of this book as I began work on it. To my surprise he actually read it (remember he was a college student and not interested in more *homework*). He then impatiently inquired, "Where's the rest of it?" It was good motivation to get back to work.

Scott, like most of us, wanted some answers. With answers, faith can grow; without answers we struggle or even give up on faith, drifting into *spiritual limbo.*

SPIRITUAL LIMBO

An unchallenged faith, once challenged, often doesn't survive and ends up on the shelf, perhaps with the abandoned childhood trinity. When young people leave home they usually enjoy their newly found freedom with less parental control. If they can also remove any *religious monkeys* from their back, they can have some *serious* fun. Having their faith challenged can serve that purpose well. Questioning or even rejecting faith gives us license to create our own set of moral rules. Some choose to operate with a better set of rules than others, and many behave better than *religious* people.

People can operate in this mode for quite some time, but life events usually trigger re-examination of their faith in God. At a personal level, it might be caused by sadness resulting from the loss of a loved one. Joyful events such as the birth of a child can also trigger re-examination. It can occur from large-scale societal events such as the tragedy of **9/11** or the bombing of Pearl Harbor.

High impact events often have a *wake-up call* effect on people, and they start looking around for answers to the big questions raised in the first four sentences of this book. Having been shocked out of *spiritual limbo,* they look for evidence of God's existence. The search is often discouraging.

IN SEARCH OF GOD

When people look for God in the obvious places – churches and religion – they're often disappointed. Instead of finding the grace of God, they often find hypocrisy: People professing one thing and doing another. They also find people quick to judge others, although the Bible teaches otherwise (Matthew 7:1-3, Luke 6:37-42). Jesus tells us not to judge, or we will be judged; not to try to remove a speck from our brother's eye when we have a plank in our own.

"The biggest problem with Christianity **is** Christians," C.S. Lewis tells us in *Mere Christianity*. You could say that about members of all religions. Some people claim a religion and then unfortunately discredit it with their behavior, i.e., Osama Bin Laden – an **extreme** example.

Seeing so much judgmental and hypocritical behavior among religious people of any faith was a major stumbling block to my achieving/receiving faith; most skeptics I talk to express the same sentiment. When religious hypocrites criticize skeptics that are good, moral people, spiritual progress often suffers for both.

Choking on Church People

Unfortunately, people within churches often *relish* being on *higher moral ground*. They seem to indulge in exercising judgment of others as if it were one of the *perks* of being religious. My wife and I both had troubling experiences with *church people* when we were young, shaping our perceptions.

When my wife was in the second grade, she attended a nearby church that she could walk to by herself. At the time, her father was a sales manager for a beer company. When the church leaders discovered this, they made a special trip to tell Smoky's mother that her daughter wasn't welcome at their church because of her father's occupation.

I experienced a less severe form of persecution as a teenager. I had a rock band that performed at teen dances; I wore my hair as long as my mother would allow. Church members disapproved of my hair length. Somehow my hair was *sinful.* I couldn't figure out why. Every artistic rendering I had ever seen of Jesus included hair much longer than mine. Later in life my friend John Vawter explained this phenomenon to be 'cultural Christianity' as opposed to Biblical Christianity. Religious people – of all religions – often confuse cultural mores or norms with spiritual values.

God Isn't a Building

I recall a scene in the story ***Roots*** where an African-American grandfather and his grandson are walking past a little white clapboard church. The grandson asks his grandfather, "How come we are not allowed to go to that church?" The grandfather replies, "Don't feel bad son, God's been trying to get into that church for years."

I was fortunate enough to meet Alex Haley, the author of ***Roots***, on January 18, 1992. I remember the exact date because we were speaking at an event and he was kind enough to autograph and date a copy of his book for me. We enjoyed a conversation: He laughed wholeheartedly when I told him we had named our cat Kunta Kitt-ay after Kunta Kinte, the lead character in his book. Alex was warm, wonderful, spiritual and vital. He died a few days later. Another *wake-up call* for a lot of people – including me.

What about Priorities?

Besides judgment and hypocrisy, many religious people set priorities in ways that don't reflect their faith. If someone *truly* believes in God and an eternal afterlife based upon this life, shouldn't that *influence* his or her priorities? For example should it influence how much time is spent on worldly pursuits vs. spiritual pursuits? On the other hand, if this life is all there is as many believe, priorities are understandably affected differently.

You may have heard the expression, "Live for today, not because life is so short, but because you are dead for so long." Yet, if I truly have an eternal perspective as opposed to a short-term perspective, i.e., after-life vs. this life is all I get, I should be motivated to use this life with eternity in mind – set priorities in a way pleasing to God. If one believes God doesn't exist, *life is* as *good as it gets*. But if one believes God does exist, *life is as bad as it gets*. People of faith and those with-out often have the same priority settings – something I didn't under-stand.

My shoulders sag when religious people drive away those who seek God with their judgmental, hypocritical and non-Biblical based behavior. These actions give validity to C.S. Lewis' point: "Christians are the biggest problem with Christianity."

Their Profession is Their Religion; Their Sin is Their Lifelessness
   Bob Dylan

The apparent *lack of joy* in the lives of those with *faith* decreased my motivation to achieve faith. If I were to turn from my *sinful* ways, I wanted to be happy about it. There are over 200 references to *joy* or *joyful* in the Bible. If God were real to these people, where was the joy talked about in the Bible? For example, Galatians 5:22-23 says, "*But the fruit of the Spirit is love, joy, peace, patience, kindness, goodness, faithfulness, gentleness and self-control.*"

With that many references, why didn't faith result in more joy for many people of faith? Turning away from worldly sins is not easy. Sin is tempting. It would help to believe whatever *pleasure* one gets from sin is to be replaced with a *true spiritual joy*; it would have helped to see it in those professing their faith.

A *joyful highlight* of my life was seeing God's creation when my children were born. It was a *spiritual rush:* My mind and body radiated with an overwhelming joy and awe. At that moment I felt connected like never before to a higher power – to God. I discovered feelings of love and selflessness that made me feel beyond human.

Witnessing the birth of my children taught me what true spiritual joy *felt* like. Though not as overwhelming, I also experienced true joy on those occasions when I did *selfless* acts of pure generosity, e.g., giving my older brother his class ring when he graduated from college. You likely have had similar experiences.

Joy is a *feeling* worth sustaining. If faith in God produces sustainable *lump-in-the-throat* joy, giving up sinful ways is a small price. However, the joy void among the allegedly faithful discouraged me.

Suspect TV Evangelists

Perhaps most troubling to my achieving faith were *some* of the TV evangelists whose sincerity seemed questionable to me. Bob Dylan wrote the song named *Slow Train Coming* (on an album by the same name) in the 1970s after becoming a Christian: The song is often interpreted as a metaphor for the second coming of Christ.

I once performed the song with a group in church. I am a mediocre musician, but church audiences tend to be more forgiving than those I performed for as a teenager. Anyway, I took poetic license with Dylan's lyrics for my church rendition and revised one of the verses to emphasize the struggle I was having with *certain* TV evangelists at the time. Below are three verses that expressed my skepticism. The first two are original to Dylan. The third is my revised verse – with apologies to Bob:

Man's ego is inflated, his laws are outdated, they don't apply no more,
You can't rely no more to be standin' around waitin'
In the home of the brave, Jefferson turnin' over in his grave,
Fool's glorify themselves, trying to manipulate Satan.
And there's a slow, a slow train comin' up around the bend.

Big-time negotiators, false healers and woman haters,
You got the masters of the bluff and masters of the proposition
But the enemy I see wears a cloak of decency
All non-believers and men stealers talkin' in the name of religion
And there's a slow, a slow train comin' up around the bend

Just turn on your television, you'll see some strange evangelism,
Just look around you, it's bound to make you embarrassed.
They ask for money on the screen, spend it in ways you never dreamed,
If they love God, how can they be so careless?
And there's a slow, a slow train comin' up around the bend.

If you follow the news, you know some TV evangelists' ungodly behavior has been exposed, including misusing donations. Criminal prosecution and jail time have resulted. At the weakest moments of my faith, I still believed *enough* that I would have been terrified to ever mock the *possibility* of God in that manner.

Safety in Silence

I have a sinful nature and I sin. At times I have felt more confident in my faith; during those times my overall behavior improved. However, in my periods of strongest faith, I had reservations about speaking to anyone on behalf of Christianity, let alone writing a book on the subject. When my faith was *stronger,* I learned to be *silent* because I had experienced *faith relapses:* I didn't want to risk *talking the talk* and then not *walking the walk.* I believe Satan gets more aggressive when you make stronger commitments to God; Satan delights in taking down outspoken believers. It serves his purposes well.

It is an *enormous* responsibility to serve God publicly. I have always been amazed that Dr. Billy Graham – arguably the highest profile evangelist in Christian history – has withstood time's test. With the nearly global free press, even a small *slip* on his part would warrant headlines.

Being Paid to Believe

Even staying above reproach doesn't ensure credibility for those employed in church or ministry work. Once your job is *dependent* upon what you believe/say you believe, your credibility can become suspect.

Unfortunately, there are some people who view a ministry as a way to 'make a living' rather than as a way to serve God; faith can have little to do with it. For example, I have seen and heard of people who, having lost their secular job, suddenly are *led* to start a ministry or work for a ministry. *Then* they start asking for financial support for a *worthy cause,* and consequently faith skeptics become at least a little, if not very, suspicious of anyone who asks for money to support a ministry.

I've had people involved in ministries cultivate a relationship with me to later ask for financial support. I wonder what their true motivation was in developing the relationship – *spiritual* or *financial?*

A particularly disheartening example of this occurred after my mother died. Correspondence from ministries she had supported while she was alive was forwarded to me. I mailed them notes explaining her death. Not a *single* ministry sent a sympathy note, but, most continued to send letters asking for money.

Exceptions – When Faith Makes a Difference

Nevertheless, I have seen meaningful changes in people's lives when they do believe in God. They're not *perfect,* but they clearly make an effort to be obedient to God. Believing God exists tends to make people more inclined to honor whatever their interpretation of God's morality, making them an exception to *typical* behavior.

Conversely, I have observed many non-believers, e.g., humanists, who behave *more* morally than many who claim themselves believers. This reinforced my skepticism of the *definitive existence* or *power* of God. If He existed, why wasn't His impact on all believers' lives more prevalent?

When I wasn't in *spiritual limbo,* I would describe myself as a *mediocre* member of the *exception group* – sort of a pathetic *wanna-be* believer. Whenever *push came to shove,* I imposed *my* will rather than any perception I had of God and I *logged off.*

Mediocre or *logged-off* believers aren't very convincing evidence – to themselves or others – of God's existence. Since they *sort of* believe, they *sort of* act like it – especially when it serves their purposes.

Some people seem to have more *devils* within them than others. There's a standard excuse you often hear for people who claim to believe, though their behavior doesn't often reflect it. People say, "Oh, he can really be (insert negative quality here), but he's a whole lot better since God came into his life."

To be fair perhaps we don't all start at the same place when it comes to our basic human nature – some have greater behavioral obstacles to overcome. Some of us seem to be tempted more by some sins than others; we all fall short of perfect.

What About the Real Exceptions?

There are *incredible* believers who seem to *program* themselves to con-tinuously *log online* to God. They are the ones who have such strong faith they never seem to question God's love or existence. Perhaps you have seen these people, usually identified by their peace, joy, humili-ty, serving attitude and fearlessness of death – even on their deathbeds.

I used to consider that if I were ever *convinced* of God's existence, I wanted to be like these people. It was the way I *desperately* wanted to be. These people had joy regardless of circumstance, remaining more content than many extremely worldly successful people I know. They were certainly more content than I was, yet often their hardships made mine pale in comparison. I would sometimes wonder, why would God allow those who love and trust Him to have such hardship?

For example, consider Ruth Evans, the mother of my best friend Jim discussed in the opening chapter. He died of a blood clot when we were 18: I can think of no greater worldly loss than to lose a child. As much as my wife and I love each other, we wouldn't hesitate to give up our lives to save our children.

Ruth didn't just lose her son: Twelve years prior, she lost her husband to heart disease. Then, after she lost her son, there was only Ruth and her daughter, Jane. Though they both could have been angry with God, they found peace. *Crucial* to that peace was that Jim and her husband believed: Jim's faith at 18 was more mature than the faith of many adults.

Some 35 years after losing her son, Ruth died. Two weeks before she died in January of 2000, I told her that one of the greatest testimonies to faith in God was the grace she exhibited during the loss of her hus-band and her son.

She smiled a gentle, knowing smile and said, "Without my faith, I couldn't have handled it. God gave me peace through those difficult times." (*Take a breath.*) Impressive!

Not surprisingly, when her time came, Ruth accepted her own death with the same grace I have observed in other incredible believers – including my mother and father.

Still a Skeptic

Ruth made me realize that people could have faith so strong that it provided *amazing grace*. But, I still doubted. My skeptical nature would prevail. You may have heard the saying, "It doesn't matter what you believe, as long as you believe." That was my concern: Believing in anything, no matter how sincerely you believe, doesn't make it true.

Psychologists Weigh In

One time a group of psychologists attended a Billy Graham Crusade to evaluate his message. In a post TV broadcast interview, they all concurred that the principles of Christianity he spoke of were psychologically sound. In particular they found the concept of God's forgiveness to be especially useful. They said people, especially those who behaved in terrible ways, need to feel they can be forgiven. Without the release of forgiveness, mental illness can result from overwhelming guilt. Consider Judas, after betraying Jesus he felt so guilty he hung himself (Matthew 27: 3-5). They also indicated that *the act of forgiving* was much healthier than harboring resentment.

The psychologists also noted that too much worry resulted in stress with adverse effects on both mental and physical health. Believing in a higher power that relieved you of your burdens, i.e., trust God to guide and protect you, would reduce worry and stress (Psalms 31: 1-5). This is a healthy thing to do: *Faith for health*.

Note the psychologists did not say God existed. They said that *believing* in the God Billy Graham spoke of could improve your mental health.

Spiritual *Down Syndrome?*

When I was a junior in high school, I went with my mother to Colorado for a year while she completed a master's degree in special education. My father, a computer scientist/physicist, remained at home so he could continue work at White Sands Missile Range in New Mexico.

While we were in Colorado, my mother and I rented a basement apartment from a family with several children, one had Down Syndrome. The diminishing effect it had on his mental capacity ironically seemed to increase his capacity for happiness. Less able to comprehend the bad in this world, he was delighted in this innocence. I can't recall him ever doing anything cruel or vicious, and little seemed to bother or embarrass him. Those who didn't consider him *normal* didn't bother him, and I used to wonder if he found more contentment in his reality than I found in mine.

Sometimes the truly spiritual people of this world don't seem to be *normal*. I am not talking about judgmental, hypocritical, *religious* people, but those who truly demonstrate *grace* above and beyond the norm. They stride through hardships that would anger, embitter or destroy *normal* people.

I was convinced their belief yielded comfort, but I didn't know if their faith was *fact* or *fiction*. I wondered if faith, even *blind* faith, could 'dupe' you to the point that you had *spiritual Down Syndrome*.

In other words, could you *create* a reality that gave you peace? Could Ruth Evans' faith have been a *make-believe* reality that allowed her to cope with an unbearable one? Was her faith in God some sort of a *spiritual lobotomy*?

In the opening chapter, I declared my skeptical nature: Perhaps I have convinced you by now. Skepticism kept me from *real* faith. My desire to have the peace of those who did believe motivated me to continue to 'seek so I could find.'

CONCLUSION

Reasons to question faith have been the focus for this chapter. For skeptics it takes solid convincing to overcome these obstacles.

To have **real** faith, you must have information you believe to build your faith bridge as discussed in **Chapter 1**. For some, little effort is required to build, but for a skeptic like me, the effort is monumental.

How do you know what is real? How can you come up with information about God you can truly believe? To answer these questions we need to understand how we can 'know what we know,' the subject of **Chapter 3**.

CHAPTER 3

HOW WE KNOW WHAT WE KNOW

This chapter was a major challenge to write. It explains in a few pages how empirical research methods are used. The material takes a little more intellectual effort and focus than previous chapters – you might want to leave the TV off while reading.

Upon completion, you will *conceptually* know more about empirical research than the typical doctoral student and many Ph.D.s. You might even enjoy hanging out with professors – if your entertainment threshold is low enough.

The tools learned in this chapter are invaluable prior to reading **Chapter 4** and especially the pivotal **Chapter 5**. When you get to those chapters you will appreciate the time invested in learning the tools discussed here. You will be able to more rigorously examine your theories and beliefs. This chapter is not directly about God, but *keep the faith:* It will help you seek Him as you complete the book.

NOTHING IS AS PRACTICAL AS A GOOD THEORY

Faith in anything is based upon what we *believe* to be true. A synonym for faith in academia would be *theory*. Most people (especially non-academics) are more skeptical of *theory* than they are of *faith*. What do *you* think of when you hear the word *theory* or *theoretical?* Most business people I ask respond to that question with answers, including ivory tower, blue sky, not practical, irrelevant or academic nonsense. In other words they don't think much of theory. They often say, "I am only interested in *practical* things, spare me the theory."

I find this reaction amusing because there actually is nothing more *practical* than a good theory. A theory is nothing more than a belief or understanding of how something works that can be tested but never proven.

Let me illustrate. If you were to pick up an object near you, a pen for instance, and pitch it up into the air, you know what will happen. First it goes up and then it falls, perhaps back into your hand if you are a good catch. You repeat the process, and it happens over and over again. You test to see if it is true of other objects: a glass, a coin, your keys. You observe that it doesn't matter what object you toss up, they all return to your hand. You are observing a pattern that is consistent. Let's say you want to test to see if the experience is unique to you. So you ask someone else to throw up the same objects. Ah hah! It is *not* unique to you.

You now have a theory: '*What goes up must come down.*' Some would even call it more than a theory; they would call it a *fact*. It is applicable to every object you have tried and with every person who has tried it. This approach is how we arrive at theories. We could go further and try to understand the reasons behind the theory, which includes yet another theory involving the scientific principles of gravity that explains why what goes up, comes down…blah, blah, blah.

CONCLUSIONS BASED UPON OBSERVATION

The above discussion is an illustration of empirical or experience-based research. It is a way to draw conclusions about 'what we know' or *believe* to be true. We may observe something ourselves or rely on the observations of others. People who conduct research in this manner are called empirical scientists. They make observations, preferably as reliably as possible, e.g., by making different observations at different times and places – *nighttime pen tossing*. They then use their reasoning skills and arrive at conclusions. In other words they use their best *logic* to assess the meaning/significance of their observations.

The fascinating thing about doing research is that you set out to answer one set of questions. Whether you answer them or not, the results of your research will usually generate *new* questions. This unceasing, unrelenting quest to learn is why research is an ongoing activity that results in a body of knowledge such as psychology, medicine and consumer behavior.

We are all at least amateur *empirical scientists*. Most of our decisions are founded upon *observation-based* theories we derive to be true about reality. For example, based upon our observation and reasoning about people's behavior, we develop theories or beliefs about people and how to relate to them, e.g., interaction with dishonest people could result in the '*you can't trust everyone*' theory.

The more correct our theories are, the more likely we are to make better life decisions. If we have incorrect theories, e.g., *my children will do as I say, not as I do*, we are apt to make poor decisions. Ideally, we would like our theories about reality to be reliable. Higher quality observations and higher quality reasoning tend to produce better development and testing of the theories we choose to believe.

Tested Not Proven

Earlier I said that theories could be *tested*. I did not say they could be *proven*. What we actually do, through experience or testing, is come to *believe* something to be true until proven otherwise. In other words we accept something to be true until it is 'disproved.' (Those readers who have conducted or are familiar with research findings know that is why hypotheses are stated in the *null* form.)

Back to the *pen toss* – is the theory that '*whatever goes up must come down*' true? Of course not. If something goes up far enough, i.e., outer space, it doesn't come back or *down*. Why something doesn't come down in this situation is explained by another underlying theory about gravity and the limits of its influence...blah, blah, blah. The point is, a theory that was held to be true for most of human existence was disproved in the 20th century when we developed the ability to make things go *way up*.

This illustrates quite well why theories cannot be proven – only rejected. The theory *"what goes up, must come down"* was universally accepted for centuries and for all *practical* purposes, was true until technology allowed things to be projected beyond the world's sphere of gravity – *intergalactic pen travel*: to go where no pen has gone before. Something can be believed to be true and later be proven false, e.g., the world was at one time believed to be flat and the center of the universe.

Believe It or Not

Accordingly, the best I can do at any point in time is to believe something is true based upon my (and perhaps others) observations combined with my ability to reason. Observations can be casual or they can be rigorously replicated scientific experiments. Clearly, the more rigorous the test, the more confidence I can have in the observation.

Using scientific research standards makes drawing conclusions more difficult. That's the bad news. Conversely, conclusions drawn in this manner are more credible. That's the good news.

CAUSALITY TRAP

One of the *slippery slopes* of conducting research is determining what *causes* something to happen. People often confuse *correlation* with *causality*. For example, just because **event B** occurred *after* **event A** doesn't necessarily mean that **A** *caused* **B** to happen. Even if *every* time **A** occurs, **B** follows, *causality* may be in question. The relationship of **A** to **B** and *possible causality* can graphically be depicted as follows:

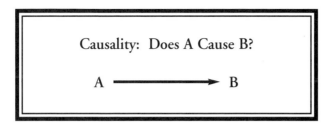

Frog Experiment

A hypothetical story used to illustrate the foolishness of mistaken *causality* is the **frog experiment**. A researcher experiments with a frog he has trained to jump every time the researcher yells, "Jump." He dissects one leg from the frog, leaving the frog with three legs. The researcher then yells, "Jump." The frog jumps but not as far.

The researcher dissects another leg and again yells, "Jump." Again, the frog jumps but hardly any distance. After removing the third leg and repeating the experiment, the frog can only slightly move by kicking his one remaining leg. Finally, the researcher dissects the last leg and yells, "Jump." This time the frog doesn't move at all.

The researcher documents in his research notes: "Sequential removal of frog's legs increasingly reduces hearing of the frog until the frog is totally deaf and does not respond to the conditioned command."

Alternative Explanations

Silly as this example is, it does make a powerful point. As long as there is an **alternative** explanation of causality, care must be taken to avoid the *causality trap.*

Journalism often falls victim to the *causality trap.* For example, I saw one headline story in a major newspaper that read, "Air Pollution is Reducing IQs of Children." The evidence cited to support this *theo-*

ry was that lower IQs were shown to exist where air pollution was higher. Those conducting the research were suggesting that since there was *correlation*, there was also *causality*. There are alternative explanations to this phenomenon that could be argued to be at least as likely as the one reported. For example, socio-economic factors of inner cities could contribute to lower IQs including lower incomes, less education of parents, substandard diets, less funding for schools, etc. Others might argue that socio-economic factors are not the cause and suggest other alternatives.

Please remember, as long as there is a plausible *alternative* explanation for a cause, care must be used in concluding *causality*. The need to consider alternatives is graphically depicted as follows:

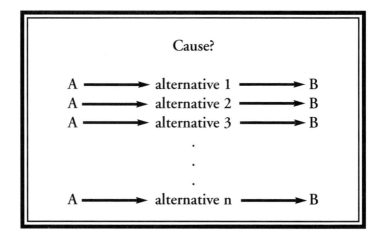

Spirituality and Causality

Caution in arriving at causality is especially tricky in the abstract arena of spirituality. We encounter people making claims that God caused good or bad things to happen.

To illustrate: when my mother was alive, she had an accident. She tripped and broke her leg during the night while walking in the dark to get a drink of water. When she told me about the accident, she pointed out that "God had let her fall close enough to the phone so that she could still call 911." With my skeptical nature I was thinking (but not saying!), "If God were thoughtful enough to make the phone handy, why did God let you trip in the first place?"

The point is, I don't know what caused her to fall, let alone fall near the phone. There are explanations I considered, but speculating was not convincing me of God's existence.

In summary, causality is not to be confused with correlation. Subsequent discussion guards against the *slippery slope* of causality, especially as we discuss how empirical research is conducted.

If this all seems too academic, remember **keep the faith**. We will put it to practical use in subsequent chapters. Your primary focus should be on understanding the *research concepts* presented, rather than specific research terminology.

RESEARCH METHODS

We use research methods to counter causality misinterpretations so that we arrive at the most reliable conclusions possible. Research methods include: *case study, sample size, time series, control groups* and *reasoning*. Each is discussed below.

Case Study

Case study is a widely used form of research. It involves an *in-depth* investigation of an individual or organization.

It Worked for Freud

Dr. Sigmund Freud popularized the case study technique by using it extensively in his psychotherapy practice. During psychotherapy, observations are made of the subject as part of the treatment. A typical scenario involves the patient completing a psychometric instrument or survey to determine what psychological problem(s) might exist – depression, for example.

As treatment for depression continues, the therapist typically has the patient complete the same instrument periodically to assess if progress is being made. In addition, the therapist would keep detailed notes of observations regarding the patient's comments and behavior. If the therapist is not satisfied with the patient's progress, modifications in treatment such as medication might be used to achieve the desired outcome. The therapist uses his or her judgment to assess what is or is not 'causing' improvement in the patient's condition. A graphical depiction of a case study is as follows:

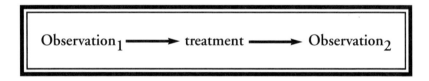

$$\text{Observation}_1 \longrightarrow \text{treatment} \longrightarrow \text{Observation}_2$$

Organizational Research

In organizational research, the case study method might be used to understand an organization phenomenon, such as a dramatic success or failure. Case study research involves interviewing organizational participants to gain insight into what happened and why. The research also involves collecting documents that reflect what was happening, e.g., turnover statistics, sales trends, profit margins or customer complaints, during the time period being studied. The usual goal of this type of research is to try to determine through judgment and reasoning what caused success or failure.

The *Harvard Business Review* is one of the top publishers of business case study research. There's a saying in business, "Try to learn from the mistakes of others; you can't afford to make them all yourself." Case studies are an excellent way to learn what can happen under certain circumstances.

Case studies can be historical, using archival data and/or the recollections of those interviewed. Case studies can also be real-time (usually called *action research*). For example, an organization might be contemplating a change in incentive systems to see what impact it has on productivity. The case researcher would collect data before, during and after the application of the *treatment,* i.e., the new incentive system.

Most business schools use case studies to teach both students and executives. They study the documented stories of real organizations, thereby providing insight into how to better succeed and avoid failure. If you think about it, studying the Bible is similar. The Bible has many stories – or case studies – of people's lives. We can learn lessons from the case studies of Biblical characters such as Abraham, David, Jonah, Joseph, Peter and Samson.

Not Conclusive

Methodologically speaking, case studies are considered to be weak in terms of scientific conclusions. They are sometimes considered to be high quality *journalism* – not real research. The primary problem is it is hard to *generalize* from a case study any certain cause and effect relationships. Case studies are particularly vulnerable to the *causality trap*. That is, you must exercise caution in concluding that because something is true in one case, it will be true in most cases or even one other case. That is why in our research on '*what goes up, must come down,*' we repeated our experiment with different objects and subjects, i.e., other tossers, rather than relying on one test with one object. Even so we came up with an *incorrect* theory.

As an example, let's say you used *yourself* as a case study after the events of 9/11. You could reconstruct your thought processes at the time and decide that you were tragically moved and saddened. Perhaps it motivated you to seek spiritual comfort. Maybe you went to church for the first time in awhile. You might *theorize* that the events of 9/11 *caused* you to go to church. Without any other information than that, i.e., you don't know that other people went to church because of 9/11, it would be presumptuous to assume that everyone responded to 9/11 the same way you did. This type of reasoning exposes you to the causality trap discussed earlier.

Nonetheless, after making a few enhancements, case study techniques are a key tool used for spiritual investigation later in this book.

Sample Size

One way to increase the confidence in your theory that the events of 9/11 caused people to go to church, would be to ask others if they experienced what you did. By asking you might find a lot of people who shared your experience. You might also find those who said that they would have gone to church anyway, but they were *more* motivated or in greater need to go as result of 9/11. There likely would be others who might say they thought about going to church more than usual but still didn't go; others might say their motivation to go to church was unaffected by 9/11. By investigating other's experiences you are increasing your *sample size*, which can be depicted as follows:

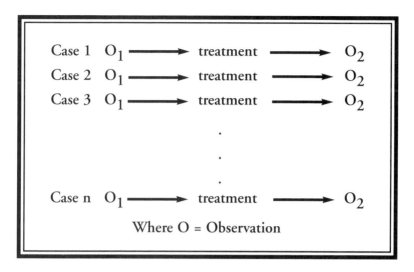

Case 1 $O_1 \longrightarrow$ treatment $\longrightarrow O_2$

Case 2 $O_1 \longrightarrow$ treatment $\longrightarrow O_2$

Case 3 $O_1 \longrightarrow$ treatment $\longrightarrow O_2$

.

.

.

Case n $O_1 \longrightarrow$ treatment $\longrightarrow O_2$

Where O = Observation

By increasing your sample size you now have more insight as to a possible theory. Based upon your sample, you have a more *generalizeable* theory. That theory might be: '*in general most people (not all) were more motivated to attend church the first Sunday after 9/11 as a result of 9/11.*' Your evidence to support this is based upon a number of *case studies* you conducted that revealed:

❖ People who *would have* attended church anyway were more *motivated* to attend.

❖ People who *wouldn't have* attended church *did* attend.

❖ Some people who *didn't attend* at least considered attending.

❖ Though some people expressed no motivation, they represented the *minority*.

There are two problems with the method described above. First, the sample is biased to people you likely have access to, which may not be representative of the general population. Second, it is time consuming to do multiple interviews.

From Case to Survey Research

An alternative to conducting multiple case studies that also allows observations to be random (and therefore minimize bias) is to conduct a survey. Survey research involves collecting data by asking for responses from a population representative of whatever the researcher is interested in studying. You undoubtedly have participated as a subject in a survey. Perhaps you have responded to a questionnaire that captured your satisfaction with a customer service experience. Survey research is the most reported type of research, and survey results are frequently in the news.

Concurrent with writing this book, I directed a research institute at Texas Tech University called the Institute for Internet Buyer Behavior. We often used survey research to determine such things as which and what quantity of products consumers were buying *on the Net* vs. at retail stores.

Survey research is a good way to get a *snapshot* at a particular time of how people feel about different issues. For example, a survey might determine how many people attend church regularly. Statistics can be used to determine how representative the sample surveyed is of the entire population. This is generally expressed in terms of survey reliability or margin of error. For example, you might hear something like, "78% of Americans were more likely to attend church after 9/11 with a margin of error of 2%."

Case Studies and Surveys are Complementary

Whether to use case studies or surveys to make observations is not necessarily an *either/or* decision. The two methods are complementary. A survey research approach allows us to get a larger sample with less effort. However, it does not provide the same rich information as an in-depth case study interview.

Often when conducting research in a new area, we first use case studies to get a deeper understanding of a phenomenon. From that we determine which questions to ask in surveys we send to a larger, more representative sample. That way we get the *depth* provided by case studies and the *breadth* provided by surveys.

Alternatively, we might be doing survey research and get some responses that we don't understand. We can then do some case study interviews to help us better understand our survey responses.

Both case study and survey research can be based upon historical events by using archival data and/or the recollections of those interviewed or surveyed. Both types of research can also be conducted in real time. Historical and real-time research techniques are used in **Chapter 5** for spiritual investigation.

Time Series

Research data (whether collected by case study or by survey) might be *biased* by factors unique to a particular point in time, e.g., taking a survey of how many people attended church the *first* Sunday after **9/11**. If you had no other observations to compare that observation to, you wouldn't know if attendance was higher or lower than before **9/11**.

However, if you had surveyed or alternatively could access historical records to determine church attendance the Sunday before **9/11**, you would see a significant increase in attendance post-**9/11**. By having observations from two points in time, you might arrive at a theory that **9/11** increased church attendance. If you had data on church attendance for the past three years and the largest spike in attendance was on the Sunday following **9/11**, your confidence in the theory increases. Time series observations can be graphically depicted as follows:

$$O_1 \longrightarrow O_2 \longrightarrow O_3 \longrightarrow O_4 \longrightarrow O_5 \longrightarrow O_6$$

9/11

Where O = multiple observations taken over time

But was an increase in attendance *caused* by **9/11** (between observations 3 and 4)? Confidence in the causality relationship is based upon three basic things:

1. Before and after information, i.e., time series observations;
2. No strong alternative explanation; and,
3. Best reasoning guides us to believe that the preponderance of the evidence supports this theory or belief.

Notice, I said *confidence* in causality, not *certainty*. Like the theory, *'what goes up must come down,'* we believe something to be true until we get a *contradictory* observation that disproves or at least makes a theory *suspect*. And since *everyone* was fooled by the *'up/down'* theory for most of human civilization, we need to be prepared to *adjust* our beliefs or theories.

Remember, we don't *prove* theories – we only *disprove* them. We develop theories based on observations and reasoning. We accept them to be true until proven *not* to be true. We have to approach our theories or beliefs about reality this way. We need to be aware that we can be fooled by the limits of both our observations and our reasoning skills. This is especially true when researching spiritual truth, which is done in subsequent chapters.

Hawthorne Studies

A classic example of being fooled comes from the *action research* project known as the Hawthorne Studies. In this research, management was trying to determine if lighting in factories would affect productivity. Their theory was that increasing *lighting* would increase productivity. In this research, *lighting* is the research *treatment* and the *outcome* or *dependent variable* being measured is *productivity*.

The *before* and *after* measures did indeed show a correlation. That is, when lighting was increased, productivity increased. Excited by the result, management increased lighting even more to see if productivity went up again. It did. It even happened a third time.

To be sure that increased lighting was *causing* increased productivity, the researchers then reduced lighting. Strangely, productivity went up again! Apparently, something *else* was causing the increase. A little deeper investigation involving employee interviews revealed the real cause: Employees were working harder because they realized they were being watched and measured. They were evidently not impacted by the lighting change. There was an *alternative* explanation. You may have experienced the effect of *measurement* if you have exercised on a machine, e.g., a treadmill, that gives you feedback on your performance. Most people indicate that their exercise effort increases when measured – even more so if certain people are *observing* them. (In health clubs, treadmill performance may even be used as a mating strategy.) Consequently, as in the Hawthorne Studies, our theory might be: '*Measurement combined with observation increases productivity.*'

In the Hawthorne Studies, the *causality* error in the lighting theory was discovered through altering the treatment and using *time series* measures. Case study interviews allowed management to get to the bottom of the issue.

Management could have been deceived easily. Had they stopped after the third observation (of increased productivity correlating to increased lighting), they would have had a false theory or belief. They could easily have pronounced their new incorrect theory and possibly convinced organizations all over the world to invest in more lighting, eventually invoking the Hawthorne *"sunglasses theory."*

Control Groups

To safeguard against being fooled as management initially was in the Hawthorne Studies, there is another useful research tool called the *control group.* The concept of a control group was first applied in agricultural research. A typical experiment would consist of taking two adjacent plots of land, planting the same type of crop, e.g., corn, and applying a treatment, e.g., fertilizer, to one crop, i.e., test group, and *not* to the other, i.e., control group. The use of both test and control groups can be graphically depicted as follows:

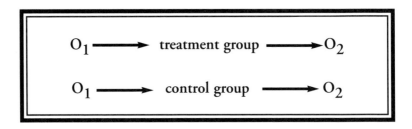

The reason for the control group is simple. We want to create an experiment where *all* things are as *equal* as possible – except for the applied *treatment.* That way, if the *treatment group* has a different outcome than the *control group*, we can have confidence that the *cause* of the difference is isolated to the treatment, or in this case, the fertilizer. If the treatment crop gets better results, we can properly credit the outcome to the fertilizer since the use of a control group has virtually eliminated an *alternative* explanation. Our theory about fertilizer is reinforced if *additional* experiments, e.g., using different geographical locations and soil conditions, produce similar results. These are referred to as replicated studies and can be graphically depicted as follows:

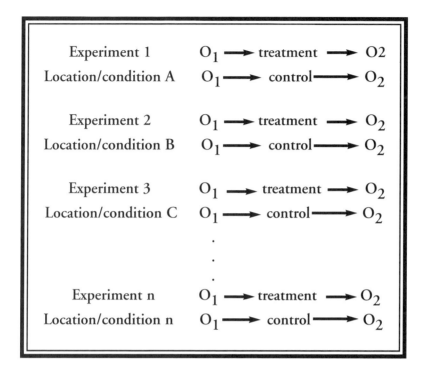

The use of a different but similar factory, as a control group in the Hawthorne Studies, would likely have revealed sooner that management had a causality problem. They could have avoided the risk of falling into the causality trap that was fortuitously averted by the use of *time series* observation. Though the lighting was *supposed* to be the treatment and thought to be causing the productivity increase, it was the act of measuring and observing that was actually having the *treatment* effect. Since the act of measuring and observing would have happened at the *control* factory (lighting unchanged), the productivity would have likely increased as it did in the *treatment* factory (lighting increased). Accordingly, researchers would have immediately known something besides the lighting was causing the increase in productivity, rather than finding out later through time series analysis.

Ideally, control groups should be as similar to the treatment group as possible. This is easier with plants than people. Once human behavior is introduced into research, the difficulty in eliminating alternative explanations for causality increases.

You probably are aware of the long, drawn out process involved in determining that cigarette smoking causes cancer. In this type of research, whether you use historical or action research, it is impossible to get truly equivalent treatment and control groups. There are so many other behaviors and possibilities that provide *alternative* explanations as to why people get cancer, e.g., pollution, genetics.

To minimize this problem, larger sample sizes are used because they are usually more representative of the population as a whole. To provide better control for alternative influences of research subjects, cancer researchers have in some experiments *substituted* rats for humans. Isolating rats in cages for use as treatment and control groups provides experimental conditions similar to those achieved in agricultural research. Of course, it can be argued that you can't draw conclusions from rats about people. But we won't go there.

It can take a lot of studies using different research designs and research subjects to reach a scientifically sound conclusion. This is especially true when a sponsor of the research, e.g., the tobacco industry, has a stake, i.e., bias, in the outcome.

An innovative research tool is used in **Chapter 5** to cope with behavioral variation control challenges when conducting spiritual research. It is called *N = 1 Experimental Design* and is discussed in that chapter.

Reasoning

Case studies, surveys, sample size, time series and control groups all play a critical role in empirical research. However at the end of the day, research observations must be interpreted. Different people can analyze the same data and arrive at different conclusions. To illustrate, witnesses or journalists often tell different versions about the same incident. As stated at the beginning of the chapter, research results often answer some questions and raise more. Research into an issue is ongoing because each discovery may result in solutions and new questions.

The highly regarded management professor and author, Dr. Peter Drucker shared an insightful example of observation, reasoning and interpretive skills. He told me about his friend, an executive of a retail chain that carries greeting cards. Drucker's friend observed that customers sometimes looked at a lot of cards before deciding, while others walked over to the cards and made a quick decision.

Most managers in the retail chain *theorized* that some people need more time to decide when selecting greeting cards. The retail executive theorized against the grain. He believed the people who made the quick decisions had looked before, shopped elsewhere and then returned after not finding anything they liked better. That explained the behavioral difference. A few interviews (case studies) validated his interpretation of the differences in behavior. He had excellent reasoning skills.

Correctly interpreting research results involves developing hypotheses about what you believe and testing them in a variety of ways. The ultimate goal is to eliminate alternative explanations until you have the one which to base your theories on. This is done through rigorous use of research methods and sound logical reasoning. That is how we 'know what we know.' Let's use these tools to investigate God's existence.

CONCLUSION

As stated earlier, theory and faith are a lot alike. In my experience many people who have faith often arrived at it with little critical thinking or testing rigor. That is why as an academic I struggled with people who claimed faith in God yet when asked, had little to base their faith on. Faith without critical examination, does not convince skeptics.

I often found these critical believers began the belief process because they wanted *to go to heaven, not hell.* Their belief gave them comfort – as would a life insurance policy. I wish it were that easy for me. My skeptical nature won't allow me to believe something simply because I *want to*, no matter how great the reward for believing. I need strong, rigorously tested proof. Getting that proof has been the greatest challenge of my life.

Using the empirical research methods discussed in this chapter and our best logic, we are collecting the information to build a *bridge* to faith that allows us to be *online* with God. In this chapter we explored how we can *know what we know.* In **Chapter 4**, we will explore how to *know when we don't know.*

CHAPTER 4

HOW TO KNOW WHEN WE <u>DON'T</u> KNOW

In **Chapter 3** we explored research and reasoning methods to help us better determine reality – 'how to know what we *do* know.' In this chapter we will explore ways to increase our insight into 'what we *don't* know.' We can raise lots of questions in this area. Some interesting spiritual questions addressed in this chapter include:

❖ Why does God allow death?

❖ Is there life after death?

❖ Why are God and His ways so difficult to understand?

The purpose of this chapter is not to prove God's existence; rather it is to allow some of the *mysteries* about the *possibility* of God to make more sense. It is a useful prerequisite to the pivotal material presented in **Chapter 5**.

SIMULATION

To explore questions about death and understanding God, we need an additional research method to add to our tool kit. This tool is *simulation* – that is, to *assume* the appearance or characteristics of reality. In research, simulation generally refers to a technique for conducting experiments in which *assumptions* about reality are made and the *outcomes* resulting from those assumptions explored.

Mortgage Loan Example

You probably use *computer simulations* often. For example, let's say you want to get a mortgage for a home you want to build. You don't know what interest rates will be when the home is finished, but you want to know *now* what the payments are likely to be. Though you *don't know* the future rate, you can still determine potential monthly loan payments using different rates and time periods *via* simulation.

You can provide a computer simulation the dollar amount and length of the loan, e.g., $150,000 for 30 years, and then provide the interest rate. Since you don't know the *actual rate*, you can enter your best guess, e.g., 8%. The simulation model could then generate a payment schedule revealing what the monthly payment would be. You can also *simulate* the effect of fluctuating interest rates on your monthly payment.

Conducting simulations in this manner allows you to experiment with *what-if* scenarios. And you can better understand the effect of different interest rates on your payment schedule. Note that you still *don't know* what the future interest will be, but you *can know* the consequences of different possible interest rates on your monthly payment.

This gives us a way to know what we don't (yet) know.

When FedEx Absolutely, Positively Needs to Know

I had the opportunity to direct the FedEx Center for Cycle Time Research at the University of Memphis in the 1990s. We used simulation models to help FedEx customers make better inventory decisions.

A key consideration in making these decisions is the trade-off between *carrying cost,* i.e., cost of inventory and storage cost vs. *shipping* costs. Our research team developed a general-purpose simulation model that would allow a decision-maker to conduct an economic analysis on this trade-off based upon assumptions about customer demand and future carrying and shipping costs.

Passenger airlines use simulation extensively to forecast revenue based upon assumptions of the number of passengers who might travel in the future to determine aircraft capacity needs and flight schedules. Have you ever been inconvenienced by an overbooked flight because of *faulty* assumptions?

As in the mortgage loan example, reality can be simulated and *what-if* experiments can determine what *could happen* even though *what will* happen is unknown. Use of simulation will prove helpful in letting us 'know more about what we don't know.' But first, let's discuss what we do know about God.

WE KNOW AT LEAST ONE THING ABOUT GOD

We may not know if God exists. However, with our basic *reasoning* skills we *do know* at least one thing *for sure* about God – either He *exists* or He *doesn't*.

Understandably there are many different interpretations, e.g., religious views of who God is. For example, my Jewish and Muslim friends don't believe that Jesus Christ is deity. They make an interesting argument that all three religions believe in one God, regardless of their interpretation of Jesus.

I'm not going to argue for one faith or religion over another. My goal is to provide the most compelling case I can for God's existence because I'm convinced that if you believe in God and strive to achieve a better understanding of Him, your life is enriched. Indeed, an excellent way to seek God and/or grow in faith is to study different religions. Such a study will help you aquire knowledge and confidence in what you embrace as your own faith. But more about that in **Chapter 6.**

Whatever your perception of God, let's see what we *find* through using simulation to make assumptions about a reality in which God *exists*.

ASSUME THIS

For centuries philosophy has employed the use of *assuming* as a technique for exploring reality, including God's existence. When you *don't know* if something is true, you simply *assume* that it is – for purposes of discussion. While operating under an *assumption*, we can use our *reasoning* skills to investigate what reality would be like if something *were* to be true, e.g., God does exist.

As stated earlier, *logically* either God *does* exist or He *doesn't*. Let's explore death, afterlife and understanding God, considering both assumptions of God's existence.

WHY IS THERE DEATH?

With or without God-faith, the *Grim Reaper* is a constant; death can bring intense grief. The bottom line: many people would prefer a death-free world, e.g., existentialists.

Consider the Alternative

Think about it; *no death*, we live *forever*. Now let's consider that alternative *extremely carefully*. *Assume* a new reality where you *never* grow old or die. This is going to take some *attentive imagination*, but work with me. You now live for eternity, which is how many people think of heaven. But there is one *huge* difference: most people's heaven perceptions are *pain/suffering* absent – a complete *evil void*.

As long as evil exists, death is ironically a necessary *escape clause* from what could be *hell* on *earth*. Though we lack the sophistication to exactly define evil, e.g., if and when to apply the death penalty, some evil extremes are abundantly apparent, e.g., serial murderers/child predators. If you really consider it, as long as there is evil – and I mean the *heavy-duty* **Hitler evil** – not having the reality of death is a *dooming proposition*.

Imagine an existence where you are subjected to the cruelty and torture of evil, e.g., Jews during the Holocaust. No matter how mercilessly you are tortured and maimed, you *literally can't die*. You might cry for your miserable existence to cease, but it won't. This simulation breeds eternal suffering – ironically a common definition of hell.

Fortunately, our human body will only take so much abuse and then we die. Death, given sufficiently intolerable circumstances, becomes a welcome gift. As unappealing as death may be, the death-free alternative is far more condemning.

Assumption Test 1

Consider the preceding discussion using the *assumption test,* i.e., assuming whether God exists. If we assume God does *not exist*, death serves the purpose of an escape clause. We may have to live in fear of death and accept loss. However, we have *peace of mind* knowing that we, and the ones we love, can never be tortured for eternity.

If we assume God *exists*, we get the same *peace of mind*, but we also get some insight into God. His provision of death shows mercy and wisdom: God set limits on worldly suffering.

The only way I want a guaranteed eternal life is if I know there is no evil, pain or suffering. That *would* be heaven.

Purge the Scourge

Beyond evil, there's another reason the *no-death* alternative remains problematic. Every seriously sick, evil person would be immortal, e.g., Hitler, Stalin, Osama Bin Laden, Saddam Hussein. That is a scary thought. Where would we keep them? Since they never die, we would accumulate more and more seriously sick and evil people.

We all begin as fairly innocent children. The evolution of evil takes time. Case studies on hideous criminals reveal they often develop a need to do *increasingly* hideous things for their evil fulfillment. If they never die, their thirst for evil would likely increase.

We could imprison the seriously evil, but now we're talking about trying to control an increasing population of evil. That is a serious *inventory* problem. What if we lost control of this enlarging evil population? And remember the persecuted cannot die. Think of war with immortal enemies, minds and ideas that couldn't die.

Death provides us with a way to purge our world of evil.

Assumption Test 2

Even assuming there is no God, death serves *purging the scourge* purposes: It plays an integral role in societal good.

If we assume there is a God, His wisdom as it pertains to cleansing the world of seriously evil people is reflected in the societal good it provides.

Wake-Up Call

Death or its possibility serves another purpose. If you've experienced the loss of death or brushed against your own mortality, you realize death has a compelling *wake-up call* effect. People appear motivated to seek life's deeper meaning and lead more purposeful lives.

As an example, the losses caused by the events of **9/11** had a noticeable spiritual effect on our nation and the world.

Though we are often inspired to be better people as a result of death, we all have a tendency to slip back into our less spiritual, less soul-searching ways. We apparently require an occasional *wake-up call* for personal or spiritual growth.

Assumption Test 3

Now that we have explored the *wake-up call* effect of death, let's evaluate death using our assumption tests.

First, let's *assume* God does not exist. In this case we can simply accept the *wake-up call* effect as a positive human experience without *spiritual* significance. From a humanist perspective, it's *nice to know* we can care but *irrelevant* to the existence of God. We might be more life mindful, adjust some priorities, e.g., spend time with the ones we love and make sure our financial matters are in order in case *we bite the dust*.

If we *assume* there is a God, then the *wake-up call* effect carries significant weight. Could it be that death is God's way of triggering *seeking* within us? It can yield that outcome.

Now you might argue, as have I, why do children die? How could God let that happen? Of course, one explanation is that as long as there is evil, death is a useful escape clause. When children are abducted, news accounts often reveal the most painful part of the experience for the parents is worrying that their child might be suffering. When they tragically lose a child, parents take comfort in knowing that any suffering was minimal. What horror if we had to fear our children could be harmed indefinitely? This again shows that under certain circumstances death can be blessing.

There is another effect resulting from the reality that *anyone* at *any age* can die at *any time*. When I was very young, I thought death was for the old. When I lost my best friend at 18, death became a *clear* and *present* danger, and that triggered *seeking* within me.

If no one died until old age, I fear most people would treat the search for God like a *term paper,* i.e., make little effort until the last minute. It is because we can lose our lives or the lives of anyone we love at anytime that creates a spiritual *awareness* or *need*. A periodic wake-up call keeps us sensitized to the possibility. This awareness usually results in more thoughtful *life prioritizing.*

But isn't that a cruel and unusual punishment for getting our attention? Not if there is indeed a superior *afterlife*. We will discuss that possibility in the next section.

Summary

Death serves three useful purposes:

1. Death provides an escape clause from evil.
2. Death purges the world of truly evil people.
3. Death can stimulate a desire to better prioritize our lives.

If there is not a God, all things considered, e.g., terrifying evil, it's better to die than to not be *able* to die.

If there is a God, the existence of death shows wisdom and mercy.

BUT IS THERE LIFE AFTER DEATH?

If there is life after death, superior to our life as we know it, then death becomes much less sinister. A useful metaphor for the transition from one existence to another is the experience of birth. Not that I remember being born, but I'll never forget seeing my children's births. As amazing as it was for me, it didn't look that pleasant for them. What if they had been asked partially through the process, "Do you want to continue being born, or would you like to go back to that secure womb where you have been living?" I am only speculating, but I suspect they would have preferred the existence that was comfortable and familiar.

Could it be that our transition from this life to an afterlife is similar? The process is difficult and fearful, but could the afterlife be far superior to this life?

The best *empirical* evidence that there is an *afterlife* comes from research based upon *near death experiences* (NDEs), including observations of those deemed clinically dead then resuscitated and statements made by individuals prior to death.

There are volumes of academic and medical research published on NDEs. You can also access a great deal of information about it on the Internet by searching under NDEs. However, Net-based information is not scrutinized like material published in research journals.

Plato (428 to 348 B.C.) is the first documentation of NDEs that I'm aware of; his writings are full of such descriptions. Plato was convinced that the soul could exist outside the physical body and would do so upon death. In Book X of *The Republic* he recounts the myth of Er, a Greek soldier who had an NDE that's strikingly similar to current recounts.

One of the best contemporary books on the subject is *Life After Life: The Investigation of a Phenomenon – Survival of Bodily Death* by Raymond A. Moody Jr. M.D. (Harper, 2001). Dr. Moody's early publications also include *Life after Life and Reflections on Life After Life*: (Mockingbird Books, 1975). His many years of work draws from experiences as a psychiatric resident at the University of Virginia Hospital where he collected hundreds of case studies (good sample size) of NDEs and found commonly observed patterns that corroborated this amazing *afterlife* phenomenon.

The common experiences included:

<u>Feelings of Peace and Tranquility</u> – Many people experience extraordinarily pleasant feelings/sensations during the early stages of death or NDEs.

<u>Being Pulled Through a Dark Tunnel</u> – This sometimes is described as a cave, well, trough, funnel, vacuum, cylinder, etc. through which they pass.

<u>Out of the Body Experience</u> – In this state, people have reported being able to observe themselves being resuscitated and describing the exact procedures used. They might look down upon their bodies from the ceiling or travel in this *out-of-body-state* to other rooms observing, and later recalling, exactly what people were doing and saying, e.g., conversations during grieving.

<u>Meeting Others</u> – Awareness of other spiritual beings has been reported. Often these spiritual beings are family or friends that have previously died, and their apparent purpose is to either assist those dying in their transition to death or to tell them that their time to die has not yet come. In the latter cases, they are told to return to their physical bodies.

<u>Being of Light</u> – An incredible element that has the most profound effect upon people is an encounter with an indescribably brilliant, bright light that usually starts dim and grows into overwhelming brilliance. It does not hurt their eyes nor diminish their sight, and the light is always interpreted as an irresistible, loving, warm and personal being. The being's identification tends to be a function of the beliefs of the person involved, e.g., Christians identify it as Christ. A panoramic view of one's entire life is often visible to both the individual and the being, as if for examination.

The being communicates through thought – not words. In a non-condemning way the being inquires something to the effect of, "Are you ready to die?" or "Have you done with your life what you wanted to show me?" Some have reported being asked questions like, "What have you done with your life that is sufficient?" or "Is your life worthwhile as you are living it?"

<u>Not Wanting to Come Back</u> – Those experiencing the NDEs obviously didn't die and *return from the dead*. Strangely, most did not want to come back, especially if they were far enough in the process to experience the light. However, if they had children, regrets or other motivations, they often wanted to return to their physical bodies.

<u>Effects on Lives</u> – People are surprisingly reluctant to talk about NDEs with people who haven't had them. However when they do, they speak of having their lives broadened and deepened. They become more concerned with moral and philosophical issues. A common lesson learned was the importance of cultivating profound love for others. None felt *righteous* as a result of the experience but had a renewed determination to live better lives.

<u>New Views on Death</u> – Though the mode of their eventual death was still a concern and they were in no hurry to die, these experiencers expressed in one way or another that "*I am no longer afraid of death.*" People who had attempted suicide reported realizing they needed

change. Ironically, there was little or no need to convince others of their experience. They were confident of their own experience and enjoyed sharing it with other *experiencers*.

Dr. Moody observed that those who had NDEs found it difficult to explain their experiences in words. But what they could express was convincing to him, and he accepted their experiences as real. The consistency within independent reports was impressive, though he acknowledged they did not constitute life-after-death *proof.*

Dr. Moody reported there are many *near death* individuals who don't recall having the experiences described above, and he has no explanation for that.

As a good researcher should, Dr. Moody reports that scientifically speaking there are alternative explanations for this phenomenon, including hallucinations, delusions, misremembering, misinterpreting and even lying. However, he accepts *life after death* as a matter of religious faith.

Within the medical community, those skeptical of afterlife argue that NDEs are the result of stimulated endorphins in the brain which – during stress – creates hallucinations similar to those caused by hallucinogenic drugs such as LSD, hashish and opium. They argue that NDEs begin and end with a dying brain. However they are unable to explain how resuscitated *brain-dead* patients have recalled specific events observed during their NDEs, e.g., recalling emergency room medical instruments and procedures, as well as conversations viewed from an *out-of-body-experience*.

Could our consciousness be like a TV program that continues to run even though the television set is turned off?

Personal Observations

You may have family, friends or acquaintances who have had NDEs as described by Dr. Moody and other academic research. If you do, that gives you stronger empirical evidence of this phenomenon.

I personally know of two NDEs from reliable sources. Ironically the first was Ruth Evans, the mother of my deceased friend Jim. She suffered from severe asthma and almost died in 1950, Jim was two; his sister was seven. The doctor came out to the waiting room, placed his hand on her husband's shoulder and told him Ruth was gone. A nurse rushed out shortly thereafter and summoned the doctor – Ruth was alive. While *near death* Ruth experienced all of the stages described in Dr. Moody's research. She also recalled coming to what appeared to resemble depictions she had seen of Jesus in the Garden of Gethsemane. The 'Jesus' entity told her that she could come now or stay. She recalls communicating that she needed to go back to raise her two children; the *coming-back* experience then occurred. She lived 52 more years! While never enjoying great physical health due to her asthma, her spiritual health was extraordinary.

The other event involved my Uncle Harry who had an NDE caused by cancer. He was an intelligent, successful man who managed a municipal airport and was not in a good spiritual place prior to his NDE. His NDE was terrifying – as some are. Afterward he became a devout Christian and spent the last five years of his life in very humble, dedicated ministry – he said he wanted to be 'ready' the next time.

Assumption Test 4

Let's now use our *assumption* technique to evaluate NDEs or the experiences of those in the process of dying. If we assume there is no God, then we should likely write off these experiences using the alternative explanation presented by Dr. Moody. They are hallucinations, delusions, misremembering, misinterpreting or lying. Though not suggested by Dr. Moody, another possible explanation is that there is a spiritual life after death without the existence of God.

If we assume there is a God, these experiences are consistent with a transition to an afterlife with a *supernatural being*. The Bible has hundreds of references to heaven in both the Old and New Testament.

There are also interesting statements about life after death. Isaiah 26:19 says, *"But your dead will live: their bodies will rise."* Daniel 12:2 says, *"Multitudes who sleep in the dust of the earth will awake: some to everlasting life, others to shame and everlasting contempt."* Paul said, *"So will it be with the resurrection of the dead. The body that is sown is perishable; it is raised imperishable."* (1 Corinthians 15:42).

Jesus tells the repentant criminal who is crucified with Christ, *"I tell you the truth, today you will be with me in paradise."*(Luke 23:43). Also of interest is that the Bible makes a clear distinction between the physical body and the soul. Jesus says, *"Do not be afraid of those who kill the body but cannot kill the soul. Rather, be afraid of the One who can destroy both soul and body in hell."* (Matthew 10:28).

Summary

I find the NDE research fascinating. It gave me great hope back in the 1970s when I first delved into it. You will recall after losing my friend Jim Evans, I was a bit preoccupied with death and my fear of it.

Comforting as this research is, I must agree with Dr. Moody, it does not prove there is an afterlife or a God. But it does encourage seeking, don't you think?

WHY ARE GOD AND HIS WAYS SO HARD TO UNDER-STAND?

As we continue our search for God, a fair question is, "Why are God and His ways so hard to understand?" Since this chapter is aimed at trying to *know when we don't know*, this is an appropriate time to explore this question.

One thing I *do* know is that I *don't* know much. I know I have quite limited mental capacity when it comes to my own existence. Just the concepts of *infinity*, *eternity* and *creation* are enough to baffle me for eternity – if I could even *understand eternity*.

One explanation I often hear is that the world and everything about it are so amazing and wonderful, God must be behind it. And a God who is capable of creating the amazing universe we live in is by definition more *awesome* than the universe. Since I understand so little about the universe, how does believing that something *even more awesome* has to be behind the universe make it any more comprehensible?

Of course the more troubling alternative is that this amazing universe happened *randomly*, i.e., there is no God. Though I was skeptical of the existence of God, I couldn't be convinced that *randomly* throwing paint against a wall for eternity would result in a magnificent painting in the Sistine Chapel.

Relative Intelligence

However there's a way I can logically deal with this dilemma: *relative intelligence*, and here's how it works. Limited as my mental capacities are, I was brilliant relative to my *infant* children. They were literally dependent upon what must have appeared to them as their *all-knowing and all-loving parents*.

Why Did You Let Me Get Hurt?

Because of their lower *relative intelligence*, infants are unaware of what is being done for their benefit and survival. I can recall taking my infant children to get their first shots. They would shriek in pain and look at their mother and me with this incredulous look of horror as if to say, "If you love me how could you let this happen?" Of course there was no way to explain the benefits of vacination.

As another example, I would tell them *don't touch the stove*, but they would touch it anyway. If it weren't hot at the time, they would conclude I didn't know what I was talking about (so much for comparative brilliance). They might touch the stove on other occasions and *empirically confirm* the *foolishness* of my rule. Then the day of reckoning came. They touched the stove when it was hot and paid the consequences of not heeding worthy *fatherly* advice and came running in pain wanting mom or dad to *make it better*.

But Why?

As my children became conversational, they learned the most *fatiguing* word a parent ever hears: *"Why?"* "Daddy, *why* does *this* or *that* do *this* or *that?*" They were merciless in their pursuit of knowledge.

Early on I could handle their elementary inquiries. But as time went on they would ask questions I knew the answer to but couldn't explain in terms they could understand – the *relative intelligence* problem. For example, one day my daughter asked me how telephones worked. I got excited – she was into my area of expertise. I started to explain analog and digital signals when she abruptly said, "Can we talk about something else?" Given her first-grade education at the time, my knowledge was useless to her. I am convinced that's why when one of her little friends asked her if her daddy was a doctor, she responded, "Yes, but not the kind who can do you any good."

It was frustrating when I couldn't explain things at a level that was meaningful to my children. It was also frustrating when they would disregard well-intended, useful advice, e.g., "Don't touch the stove, stay away from that plant – it's poison ivy." It seems when told not to do something – that something becomes more tempting.

Imagine God's Intelligence

Imagine that *relatively* speaking, God is at least as much greater in intelligence and mental capacity than we are relative to infants. That's not a hard assumption to make given how little we know compared to what *we could know.*

There is even some empirical evidence for the notion of a much higher level of intelligence. Though not as common to most 'near death' experiences, there are reports of people saying that during their encounter with the *being of light* that they had a profound experience of *knowing.* Things that had never made sense before became perfectly simple and clear. They report they can't recall the knowledge, but they remember experiencing it. They wish they still had it.

There is Biblical support for this notion of relative intelligence as well. Throughout the Bible, God is represented as an *incredible source of wisdom,* e.g., 2 Chronicles 9:23, Job 9:4, Psalms 51:6, Proverbs 1:2 and 7, Acts 6:10 and Romans 11:33.

If I Only Knew Then

You have probably heard the expression, "If I knew then what I know now," when people wish they could relive a part of their younger years. That expression has some applicability to the concept of relative intelligence.

One of the hardest things I ever did was leave my daughter at a day care center for the first time. She did not want to go. She cried, "Daddy please don't leave me!" She had the most desperate look in her eyes. I knew she would be fine. If she *knew then* what *I knew*, she would've been fearless. But nothing I could say or do could convince her. When I was able to muster up the emotional strength to leave, she genuinely felt I had abandoned her.

As a doting father, I called several times to check on her. She was fine, and had no problem the next time I left her. But that *first* time, her mental capacity could not process the idea that everything would be all right. Though she couldn't *know* what I *knew*, if she would have had *faith* in what I told her, she would have been comforted.

If God is exponentially greater in *knowing*, when we have our adult equivalent *nursery school* crisis, does He patiently know it will work out fine? We just need a *growth* experience or perhaps *we* need more *faith*. Could the loss of loved ones not be a real tragedy? If they go to an exponentially more wonderful existence with God, are they not better for the loss of this life? Will we not be better for the loss? But when we can't comprehend or understand – we fear the unknown.

Assumption Test 5

If we assume there isn't a God, the relative intelligence perspective has no meaning. Any assumptions about His relative intelligence are irrelevant.

If we assume there is a God, the notion of *relative intelligence* provides some profound explanations. Let's add to the assumption that not only is God exponentially more knowing, He is also exponentially more *loving*. Think of the love a parent has for a child. Now imagine that kind of love increased exponentially as God's love for you.

A God with knowledge, wisdom and love so great we can't comprehend. It is an amazing assumption to consider. What can we learn from this assumption?

Q & A With God

Let's ask some of life's questions and *imagine,* if you will, what God's answers might be. This hypothetical *Q & A* is based upon answers I might give my adult children as their father.

Q. Why can't we have total freedom?

A. God knows that what we want is not always what's best for us. Because He loves us He wants what is best for us, even though we might not understand it at the time. Is a train more free on or off the tracks?

Q. Why do we get hurt?

A. God doesn't want us to hurt. He allows us to make decisions, i.e., free will. If we make bad decisions, they often have hurtful consequences. Sometimes, like when we allow our children to experience hurt from medical procedures, God allows us to experience hurt because it might be necessary or useful for our spiritual health.

Q. Why is evil allowed?

A. God doesn't want evil, but human choice yields the *opportunity* to do evil. Would you want your children to willingly love you or to love you because they were *forced* to do so? Is it not more meaningful when they *choose* good over evil? If everyone made *good* decisions, evil wouldn't exist. Think how *heavenly* wonderful that would be.

Q. Why do we have to follow rules and commandments? They often don't seem relevant or culturally current.

A. God wants you to be obedient for your own good. His rules are and have always been relevant, and they will protect you from bad decisions. If you break God's rules it hurts both you and Him, it puts distance between you and God and weakens your faith. God allows you freedom to break His rules. When you do, He prefers that you realize your errors and repent; for that reason God is patient. God, like your parents, loves a repentant heart. And like a parent, God will not allow continued disobedience. You may be punished. But remember, when you acknowledge your wrongdoing and ask for forgiveness, God forgives.

Q. How do we make righteous or good decisions?

A. God placed within us a conscience that guides us to truth and directs us away from evil, e.g., Romans 2:1-7. Even without God's word, this conscience gives us a sense of right and wrong and of fairness in dealing with others. The evidence of this conscience is in the moral codes of conduct documented in ancient Roman, Egyptian, Greek and Chinese civilizations. Today, you find it apparent in different civilizations and religions where there are common attitudes about acceptable and decent behavior. For example, cowardice, murder, lying, stealing, selfishness, greed, corruption, adultery and cheating are rarely revered cross-culturally. Love, forgiveness, generosity, humility, compassion and selflessness are usually admired.

Q. Does God get angry?

A. God is like a parent. When your children fail, are you more angry or more heart broken? If punishment is warranted, does the punishment hurt you more than your children? Does your punishment seem like anger when in reality it is a loving attempt to change behavior that is destructive?

Q. Why are there so many things like infinity and eternity that seem incomprehensible?

A. Be patient. Things that don't make sense now will make sense later.

Q. Why do we need to pray?

A. God is the source of wisdom and knowledge. He knows what is best for us. He can better communicate His wisdom and knowledge if we converse with Him in prayer. If we pay attention He answers our prayers, maybe not by giving us what we want but by giving us what is best.

Assume there is a God with *perfect* knowledge, wisdom and love wanting to answer your questions, to guide, to comfort and to love you. Wouldn't you want to be *online* with Him?

CONCLUSION

The purpose of this chapter was to learn more about things we don't know. Through the use of assumptions, we explored why we die, if there is life after death, and why God and His ways are hard to understand. We learned the answers to these perplexing issues vary greatly depending on whether we assume that God exists or He doesn't.

We didn't *prove,* nor were we trying to *prove* that God exists. I hope this discussion was enlightening and, more importantly, *encourages* you to want God to exist. In the next chapter, I will share with you the way God gave me the gift of faith. If you do not yet have that gift, **Chapter 5** presents a way to receive it.

CHAPTER 5

THE GRAND EXPERIMENT

This is the pivotal chapter of the book. In this chapter we will draw upon the building blocks we have developed in the previous chapters. We will use the Internet metaphor, empirical research techniques, reasoning, simulation or assumption testing and conduct the *grand experiment*. Along the way I will bear my soul – just a little.

RESEARCH TECHNIQUES REVISTED

You will recall in **Chapter 3**, we talked about the use of case studies, sample size, time series and control groups as ways to strengthen the validity of our observations. Through the use of these techniques, we'll try to improve our *reasoned interpretation* of *causality* and eliminate *alternative explanations* to what we believe to be true, e.g., we don't want to be duped as in the Hawthorne Studies.

A key research technique used to eliminate alternative explanations is the *control group*. Unfortunately in the real world of research, it is a major challenge to *truly* get equivalent *test* and *control* groups for human behavior-based experiments. You will recall the notion of test and control groups came from agriculture and how much easier it is to get equivalency when you are dealing with plants instead of people. People have great variance in their physical and psychological make-up. This variance can unduly bias research results. There is a straightforward research solution to address this problem, referred to as $N = 1$ *Experimental Design*.

N = 1 Experimental Design

N = 1 Experimental Design uses only *one* subject; that one subject is used in both the control *group* and treatment *group*.

Here is how it works. Let's pretend you want to empirically evaluate the effect of a particular diet on your weight and body fat. Using a *time series* approach you could measure your weight and body fat once a week for 12 weeks *before* you go on the diet.

Then you go on the diet for 12 weeks while taking weekly measurements of your weight and body fat. You try to keep everything else about your routine the same, e.g., you don't increase or decrease your exercise routine. *After* several weeks your weight has dropped 10% and your body fat has dropped 8%. This change indicates possible *causality,* i.e., the diet has *caused* the weight loss and body fat reduction. Now you return to your former eating habits for 12 weeks and repeat your weekly weight and body fat measures. If at the end of the 12-week period you have regained your original weight and body fat, our interpretation of causality is convincing.

You can repeat the diet *treatment.* If the weight and body fat loss you achieved previously occurs again, you have *reasonable* evidence that the diet reduced weight and body fat.

In case you missed it, you have been *both* the *treatment* 'group' and the *control* 'group.' When you are on the diet you are the treatment group; when you are not on the diet you are the control group. Each time you go off and back on the diet, you are replicating the experiment. Replication of results increases confidence in your conclusion of the *reality* that the diet causes weight and body fat reduction. Replication is graphically depicted as follows:

$$O_1 \text{---control---} O_2 \text{---treatment---} O_3 \text{---control---} O_4 \text{---treatment---} O_5$$

Where O = Observation

What About Sample Size?

In **Chapter 3** we discussed the importance of sample size to increase our confidence in research results. How does this work in the *N = 1 Experimental Design*? We ask *others* to conduct the same experiment; if we get similar results we can *generalize* that this diet works for most people.

In other words, we increase our sample size by collecting multiple N = 1 design experiments.

Other Applications

You can see how the *N = 1 Experimental Design* could be used to study a number of treatments using yourself as both treatment and control group. For example, you can test an exercise program, medications – or the existence of God – as we will demonstrate shortly.

belief in

HISTORICAL APPLICATION

We mentioned in **Chapter 3** that research can be either historical or action oriented. In historical research we use archival data and recollections of past events. A particularly well-regarded example of historical research in business is the best selling book *Built to Last* by James Collins and Jerry Porras (Harper Business 1994).

Built to Last

The book's purpose is to document how *premier* or *visionary* companies outperformed other companies during a sustained number of decades. *Outperformed* means their stock prices surpassed their comparable rivals an average of 6 to 1 over multiple decades. The rivals were not losers. Rather they were all successful companies with stock prices outperforming the general stock market 2 to 1 which means the *premier* companies' stock prices outperformed the *general stock* market 12 to 1!

The premier companies are considered the *treatment group* for the purpose of the study. The *treatment* is whatever contributed to their beating the market odds. In fact determining the *treatment* or the *cause* of the incredible performance was the target of investigation. The *control group* consisted of the successful (but not as successful) companies that were *competitors* to the companies in the *treatment group*.

For example, a treatment group company such as Johnson and Johnson had as a control group the company Bristol-Myers Squibb. Marriott had as a control group Howard Johnson. Procter and Gamble had Colgate as a control group. Boeing paired with McDonnell Douglas, etc.

Over a six-year period the authors rigorously investigated the history of each company to determine what was consistently different among the overachievers and the less successful companies. They found that unlike the control companies, premier companies are not primarily focused on *beating* their competition; they are more inclined to *compete with themselves* in search of ways to improve – to be better tomorrow than they are today. (Perhaps applicable to our personal/spiritual growth.)

Also premier companies, unlike less successful companies, don't make profit maximization their primary focus. Premier companies do seek profits, but they are equally guided by a core ideology – a sense of purpose beyond just making money. Paradoxically, they are more profitable than profit-driven companies.

Many of the companies in the study were more than 100 years old. In century old or older companies, research revealed even greater insight into what it took to have real *staying power* in the competitive business world. Company longevity requires changes in leaders with the passage of time. Two observations about attributes of leaders in premier companies are insightful:

❖ First, being a charismatic visionary leader was not required. The leaders of premier companies strive to be *clock builders*, not *time tellers*. Their focus was long-term as opposed to instant gratification.

❖ Second, these CEOs were almost exclusively drawn from *inside* the company.

Are We Built to Last?

Using the *N = 1 Experimental Design* technique, we can do some historical research on our lives. Outcomes of this research might be as insightful as they were in the ***Built to Last*** research.

In my experience, most people at one time or another feel at least some type of God connection, whatever their interpretation of God may be. Some people are brought up in a faith that results in that connection. It might also be the result of a significant incident in their lives, such as the birth of a child or the loss of a loved one. Sometimes, it results from just seeking God in an effort to find meaning to life. The result of that *connection*, however strong, might eventually lead a person to a strong faith. At the other extreme, it might have little or even a negative spiritual effect and may result in rejection of God.

As a tragic negative example, Hitler was brought up in the Christian faith and at one point planned to be a priest. As an adult he rejected Christianity as a faith of weaklings: Hitler believed that the German race was superior and by keeping it pure through avoiding marriage to Jews and Slavs, German children would then be born in *his* image of God. This thinking contributed to the Holocaust and the murder of some six million Jews and other innocent people.

Often people fluctuate somewhere in between agnosticism and weak faith. Many people have told me, whether they believe in God or not, there were times when they experienced something that could be described as spiritual. Maybe it can be described as a longing or need for God. For some people this longing was observable after the tragedy of **9/11**.

In your own personal history, consider feeling connected or believing in God as a *treatment* effect. Consider not feeling connected to God as a *control period* in your life. Using the Internet metaphor, sometimes you might feel *online* with God and sometimes you might feel *logged off.*

If you have never had a sense of wonder or any type of *God-connection* the following investigation may have no meaning. Feel free to skip it and go to the next section, although reading it may still be instructional.

Investigate Yourself: Online vs. Offline

I have found it useful, as have others, to examine one's life and evaluate what differs during the *treatment* period vs. the *control* period. This self-examination, of course, is a personal experience for your personal evaluation.

An interesting as well as useful way to evaluate the *God-connection treatment* is to look at it from a *decision-making* perspective. The human experience can be viewed as making one decision after another. There are big decisions such as who to marry, what career to pursue, and how to respond to a teenager who breaks the rules. There are small decisions such as what to wear today, what to eat for lunch, and how to respond to that *idiot* who aggressively cuts you off while driving. As part of your evaluation, are there any differences in your decisions – big or small – when you are *under the influence* of God? Do you feel you make better decisions when God influences you? Is your conscience more active during the *treatment* or the *control* periods?

Another interesting way to evaluate the *treatment* effect is to consider your sense of comfort and peace. C.S. Lewis ironically observed that if you seek truth you will find comfort, but if you seek comfort you will not necessarily find truth. A compelling argument often made by those who believe in God is that many people *don't want to believe in God* because it will require a *change in their lifestyle.*

What about your relationships? Do you get along better with family, friends and co-workers when you are *online* with God? If married, is your marriage positively influenced when you are *online* with God? A graphical depiction of your investigation might look like the following:

O_1 Control ⟶ O_2 Treatment ⟶ O_3 Control ⟶ O_4 Treatment

Where O = Observation of:
Quality of decisions about life
Sense of comfort and peace
Quality of relationships

Control = times you were more offline from God
Treatment = times you were more online with God

My Investigation

I share some of my investigation in hopes that it might be useful to you. As I pointed out in **Chapter 2**, I spent much of my life in *spiritual limbo,* being a person of *weak faith* and living a 'status quo' lifestyle.

My parents never really approved of my rock musician phase – mostly the lifestyle troubled them. At one point they used a *tough love* strategy and told me if I wanted to pursue my rock music, I was on my own. Not letting my lack of talent stand in the way, I was independently putting myself through college at age 19. I was poor much of the time and sometimes went hungry.

And I learned to be self-sufficient. Others relied on me; I relied on no one. Self-sufficiency results in independence and pride that does not lend itself to obedience to a higher power. I began to believe that faith in God was a crutch for the weak or a ruthless weapon of the self-righteous.

I considered myself moral *where it mattered to me.* This can lead to *self-deluding* moral relativism where one is *selectively moral.*

Most people are not tempted by *every sin* or *vice.* For example, drugs or alcohol do not tempt me. Accordingly, avoiding overindulgence in these areas is no credit to me or evidence of my obedience to God.

However, I seem to compensate for those *non-temptations* by *lacking* good impulses in *other* areas where I have made bad decisions – areas where I *am* tempted. I began to make *my own rules* that resulted in poor *decisions,* bad consequences and feeling *offline.* When I was feeling connected to God, however, I made wiser decisions.

In **Chapter 1**, I mentioned my year of Bible study and the trip to the Holy Land during my intense seeking stage. Not since being a child had I felt so connected to God. It was a joyful feeling similar to the *awe* I felt when my children were born. I was committed to serving God in some way.

But things in my life didn't go as I expected. I felt I had committed to God but foolishly expected that would result in the reduction of life's problems. I should have paid more attention to the story of Joseph in the Bible. He was committed and loyal even when the world turned against him – far beyond anything I was struggling with during my faith crisis.

I have since learned that faith doesn't eliminate worldly problems and struggles, e.g., Ecclesiastes 9:11 and Matthew 5:45. If it did, faith would be a great bargain and readily taken by all. What faith does instead is allow you to live in grace through life's problems and struggles. By striving to make *godly* decisions, you will at least reduce those problems you bring upon yourself.

At any rate, during my struggles I became discouraged and foolishly went *offline* from God. I decided to rely on my stubborn self-sufficiency – solve my problems my way. Looking back, I could have avoided many bad decisions I made during those years. Though successful in worldly terms, I was a spiritual failure.

Summary

Although not rigorously controlled research, historical research using *N = 1 Experimental Design* reveals a great deal to me about my life during times of being *online* or *offline* with God. I hope this approach is helpful to you. Let's see what we can learn by moving from historical research to action research.

ACTION RESEARCH

A good way to appreciate how action research works with *N = 1 Experimental Design* is to actually conduct your own research. To get started I want to share a story and a poem with you. The story is about my mother and my two daughters.

My Mother's Story

To a person with faith in an afterlife with God, death *can* be an adventure to which one looks forward. Death is the ultimate *litmus test* of a person's faith. It was for my mother – and it was a test she gracefully passed. She was convinced she was going to be with God and with family members who had passed on before her. In the spring of 1996, she was told she had six to nine months to live; she was dying of colon cancer.

She not only accepted her fate with grace, she literally *seized* the moment to demonstrate to family and friends the comfort God provided her. When guests would come to visit her, they would be a little timid; reluctant about what to say. Those without faith were often awkward as they entered her home and tried to initiate friendly conversation. They didn't know what to expect, but they didn't expect her to be *cheerful*. She was.

My mom and I made sport of these situations and came up with a totally *disarming* welcome for her guests. I had ridden a Harley Davidson motorcycle from Minneapolis to her home in Albuquerque so I would have transportation while I spent time with her during her remaining months. When we knew someone was coming by, my mom put on my black leather gauntlet motorcycle gloves and a black leather skullcap I picked up for her at the Harley dealership. She topped off her ensemble with a pair of black wrap-around sunglasses.

I wish you could have seen her. There she sat, a frail, pale and fading, sweet woman in a nightgown wearing this *Harley get-up*. As guests would cautiously peer into the room, she would pleasantly startle them by demanding, "You get in here and give me a hug!" Talk about an icebreaker!

People came to comfort her but left comforted. Those of faith, reassured. Those without faith, a little more motivated to seek. It was my mother's finest hour. You may have heard the saying that the reward for a good life is a good death. My mother was empirical evidence of that. We all miss her, but her faith made her loss easier to take – less tragic.

Jessie's Music and Jamie's Poem

We had a service to celebrate my mother's life. We asked Jessie, my younger daughter, to play the piano. She had done the same without missing a single note eight years earlier at the celebration of my father's life. Jessie was only seven when her grandfather died. They had a special relationship that involved much playful laughter. Her mother and I were surprised when she asked to play at his service – we thought she might be too young. We weren't concerned about her talent; her skills far exceeded her age. I will never forget her performance. This petite little seven year old climbed up on that piano bench and *blew everyone away*. Now at fifteen, we had no doubts she could play masterfully for her grandmother's service – and play she did.

My older daughter, Jamie, was seventeen years old at the time her grandmother died. She is a writer whose ability to express herself is far better than mine. I asked her to write a poem to be included in the program and read as part of the celebration. It captures the essence of the loss we all felt:

In Loving Memory
of
Marguerite C. Wetherbe

March 14, 1920 – November 14, 1996

She died somewhere in between a Thursday and a Friday
But she should have died at the lazy hour of three o'clock
On a Sunday afternoon
When the hot New Mexico sun stings cactus roses
And the lizards rest on vacant park benches
And every body walks slower

And when she died she took this perfect ginger bread
Cookie-cutter shape right out of my soul
The cutter filled with nutmeg and cinnamon
She took rusted-out swing sets, homemade water slides,
And small forts hidden behind lilac bushes and clothes lines

She was as wholesome as strawberry and cream oatmeal
Made from scratch on an open stove,
And she was made up of something
That special something that gives turquoise a blue-green color
And whatever makes a watch crystal reflect a rainbow
Onto plain bedroom walls
And her hands were dramatically creased but softer than mine
My hands look barely used next to hers

And now, all I'm left with are random images
and our matching skin color.

Jamie Wetherbe
November 1996

I have never been able to read that poem without being emotionally overwhelmed. I can't read it aloud because the 'throat god' puts a lump in my throat that renders me speechless. It amazes me to this day that my wife was able to read it at the celebration service to family and friends.

Were you moved? Did the reading of my Mother's story and Jamie's poem touch you in an *emotional* perhaps *spiritual* way? Then consider the reading of the story an *action-research treatment* where *you* are the research subject. Consider how you felt *before* and *after* you read the story and the poem.

Assumption Test

Being moved doesn't prove the existence of God any more than a sentimental movie or novel that moves you proves anything *spiritually*. However, let's explore your response (or the outcome) from the story/poem treatment using the assumption test technique.

First, let's *assume* there is *no* God. In that case we can simply write off the *moving* experience as a human experience with no *spiritual* significance. If we assume there is a God, could emotional or spiritual experiences be His way of connecting to our souls? It certainly takes us to a higher plane of being human.

Plato Weighs In On Mystical Experiences

Plato, one of the greatest thinkers of all time, strongly believed in the use of reason, logic and argument to attain truth and wisdom. However, he felt there were limits to that approach. He also suggested that ultimately truth might come to one in an almost mystical experience of enlightenment and insight. He believed there were planes of higher reality. These planes were beyond the reasonable, logical ones limited to us in this life.

I would like to share a mystical experience with you. If you don't think it mystical, perhaps you will agree it is at least good *chicken soup for the soul.*

I have had several people of exceptional faith in God tell me that God communicates in mysterious ways – but you must be listening.

My wife and I had moved from Minneapolis back to Albuquerque. We had become empty-nesters and wanted to return to New Mexico. We started attending the church I went to as a child with my friend Jim Evans. It's a large church with thousands of members. At the first service I was surprised to notice they did not have a piano, because large churches usually have a grand piano.

After the service, I went up to the music director and asked about the piano situation. He explained that the soundboard in their old piano had cracked rendering it useless. They were going to replace it but currently didn't have the resources.

Here Comes a Piano

Shortly after that conversation, I felt this deep down feeling that my wife and I should replace the piano. Whenever I thought about it I would get a version of that radiating joyful feeling I got when my children were born: It felt simultaneously unselfish and wonderful.

The following week Ruth Evans died in Oklahoma where she had lived with her daughter until her death. Ruth was a charter member of our Albuquerque church when it was founded 50 years earlier. I felt moved to donate the piano in her memory. I called Jane, her daughter, to tell her the story and ask her permission to donate a piano in her mother's name. After hearing my request Jane, a real *onliner,* said, "How strange. I had forgotten all about it until you just mentioned the piano, but when my father died my mother received $10,000 from my father's life insurance policy. She used a portion of it to buy a piano for the church." Nearly fifty years earlier, Ruth had felt moved to donate a piano to the same church.

A *spiritual rush* went right through me. "Awesome," I whispered to myself. **Chapter 1** described Dr. Phil's observation that sometimes God will nudge you trying to get your attention. If that doesn't work, he will eventually drop a piano on you. This was both *literally* and *spiritually* a *grand piano* experience for me – a positive one. Was it a random coincidence, e.g., like how some believe we came into existence? Or was this a little gift from the *Man with a Plan*? I believe that in a loving, playful way, God was revealing more of Himself to a perpetually seeking soul. It was as if He were confirming once again – *I do exist*. In my perpetual seeking, I had responded to a spiritual feeling that He placed within me, to *donate the piano*. He responded in a compelling way. What convinced me? *I was there*.

Replication is Key

I do not base my faith in God on this single unique experience for which any skeptic could provide an alternative explanation. I am basing it upon *replication* experiences of this nature. They are not uncommon when you learn how to stay *online* with God. He talks to you if you *listen*.

> *Some listen and receive,*
> *Some practice to deceive*

Steele Croswhite

At this point, I realize that there are *two types* of readers. First there are those who have experienced being *online* with God and they know about these experiences. The second type of reader has not had such experiences and is understandably skeptical of their reality. If you are in the latter group, as I used to be, the simple yet very demanding *spiritual experiment* discussed below will I hope be meaningful for you.

SPIRITUAL EXPERIMENT

Are you ready to participate in a *spiritual experiment?* In case you need just a little more convincing, please consider this: In 1980, if the Internet had been described to you, would you have written it off as futuristically unbelievable?

It is *difficult* to believe something until you *experience* it. Please keep that in mind as I describe the *N = 1 Experimental Design*. It is a refined version of the one I used to get *online* with God. But first, a little background to provide useful context and to legitimize the approach used in the experiment.

God Don't Make Promises He Don't Keep
Bob Dylan

To set the stage for the experiment, I am paradoxically referencing the Bible and arguing that it is not necessary to have access to the Bible to find God. The Bible is the best selling book of all time. To ignore it in our search for God would seem foolish. On the other hand, not everyone has access to the Bible. Accordingly, a God that only allows you to be online with Him if you have Bible access is arguably unfair.

Let's look at what the Bible says about finding God starting with Jeremiah 29:13, *"You will seek me and find me when you seek me with all your heart."* That promise is especially meaningful because it states you can *successfully* seek and find God without ever having heard of the Bible or Jesus Christ.

Logically, I could never understand a God that requires you to be instructed by other humans, e.g., formal religions. A fair God would hold you accountable for what you know. In other words, if the Bible is from God, it should assist you in your spiritual walk. If you don't have access to the Bible or its teachings, this should not exclude you from accessing God.

The Bible speaks to this issue often and fairly. Consider Romans 1:20, *"For since the creation of the world God's invisible qualities – his eternal power and divine nature – have been clearly seen, being understood from what has been made, so that men are without excuse."* In other words. we have a God *consciousness* within us. We either respond to it or we reject it *regardless* of our access to religious resources. To seek God we must respond to our God consciousness. Psalms 10:13 says, *"Why does the wicked man revile God? Why does he say to himself, 'He won't call me to account?'"*

C.S. Lewis described God consciousness in **Mere Christianity** as follows:

> *These, then, are the two points I wanted to make. First, that human beings, all over the earth, have this curious idea that they ought to behave in a certain way, and cannot really get rid of it. Secondly, that they do not in fact behave in that way. They know the Law of Nature; they break it. These two facts are the foundation of all clear thinking about ourselves and the universe we live in.*

That was written more than 50 years ago. To illustrate the universality of Lewis' observation, consider the following Cherokee Indian parable:

> *An old Cherokee Indian was telling his grandson about a fight that goes on inside himself. He said the fight is between two wolves. One wolf is evil: anger, envy, sorrow, regret, greed, arrogance, self-pity, guilt, resentment, inferiority, lies, false pride, superiority and ego.*

> *The other wolf is good: joy, peace, love, hope, serenity, humility, kindness, benevolence, empathy, generosity, truth, compassion and faith.*

The grandson thought about it for a minute and then asked his grandfather, "Which wolf wins?"

The old Cherokee simply replied, "The one I feed."

An important aspect of seeking God is to respond to the goodness within us. Romans 2:7-8 tells us, *"To those who by persistence in doing good seek glory, honor and immortality, he will give eternal life. But for those who are self-seeking and who reject the truth and follow evil, there will be wrath and anger."*

The Bible is clear that the observance of religious laws is not the path to God, *faith is.* Romans 3:28 states, *"For we maintain that a man is justified by faith apart from observing the law."*

Some religions get quite proprietary and monopolistic in their claims to be the *only way* to God. That seems extremely self-serving and perplexing to many in search of God. Different religions can't make *exclusive* claims *and* all be correct. These *hair-splitters* would have you believe a seeking soul is kept from God on a *religious technicality.* It's sad we can't find challenge and discovery in sharing our *God path* differences rather than becoming judgmental.

Paul goes on to instruct us in Romans 12:3, *"Do not think of yourself more highly than you ought, but rather think of yourself with sober judgment, in accordance with the measure of faith God has given you."*

In summary, anyone who truly seeks God in earnest can find him with or without the use of Biblical or other religious teachings. They simply need to respond to their God consciousness and seek God earnestly. God will respond. However, just as some are given more talents in some areas than others, *faith* comes more easily to some than others.

It never came easy to me. My analytical, logical, skeptical, stubborn brain got in the way. I also learned I was seeking with *insufficient commitment*. Too often, I would say to God, "If you exist, reveal yourself. In the meantime I will go on about my business *my* way." When I finally made a *heartfelt commitment*, God kept his promise.

It is this *heartfelt-seeking process* I share with you in hopes that it will be helpful.

It Begins with the Experience

To know God, *to be online with Him*, is an incredible *experience*. What we need is *that experience* of God's presence to know he exists. My earlier *weakling* attempts at faith in God were not *worthy* of that experience. I got glimpses of Him – those were enough to keep me curious but never satisfied. A real *online* connection requires the appropriate effort. Here is how you can do it:

1. Make your best effort to believe God exists. If you can't do that at least assume He exists. If believing in God as a *being* is too much of an intellectual stretch, believe in the concepts of love, mercy, forgiveness, wisdom, honor, truth, joy, peace, humility, generosity and compassion. Isn't this what the essence of God represents?

2. Think of some of the most wonderfully emotional (or spiritual) feelings that you have ever experienced. For me, two of those experiences were when my children were born. Other times include generous acts to those in need. Recall the radiating, joyful feeling you experienced during those times. Consider that feeling to be a benchmark for doing something of which God approves.

3. Think of the worst feelings you have had about yourself. Think of times you have done despicable things that you

would prefer no one know about. Maybe it was something motivated by greed, envy, lust, foolishness, hate or revenge. Consider these shameful feelings as a benchmark for being ungodly or being influenced by evil.

4. Take the extremes of the *Ungodly* and *Godly* feelings and place them (and words you might associate with them) at the ends of a continuum with the center of the scale being considered NEUTRAL as illustrated below:

Ungodly		Godly
regret/dispair------------------N------------------------joy/peace		
hate/revenge--------------------E----------------love/forgiveness		
arrogance/pride----------------U------humility/servant attitude		
greed/envy----------------------T--------generosity/compassion		
foolish/worldly-----------------R--------------------wise/spiritual		
deceit/lies----------------------A----------------------honor/truth		
failure/self-pity----------------L---------------------victory/hope		

You will recall that earlier in this chapter, the human experience was viewed as "making one decision after another." For purposes of the *N = 1 Spiritual Experiment*, anytime you make a *decision* that tips *how you feel* toward the G*odly* side of NEUTRAL, consider that as following God's will and therefore pleasing to God. Do the same with decisions on the other side of the equation. You can think of this process as doing a **God check** or seeking **God guidance** before making a decision.

Let the Experiment Begin

Please take an observation on your feelings about the following:

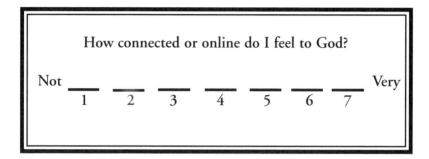

Now that you have a *baseline* observation, we are ready for the *treatment*. I ask you to pray (or if you prefer, to meditate) about God's existence. You can pray something as simple as:

> *God, I am seeking You with my most sincere, heartfelt effort. Please reveal Yourself to me in convincing ways. In my effort to connect to You, I will be obedient to what I believe to be Your will. I commit to yield my will to Yours.*

Once you have made your prayerful request of God, make your most sincere effort to honor your commitment to Him. Do that in the way you *make decisions*. As you make them, seek God's guidance or influence. Consider yourself *online* with God. With your *inner voice* ask God, "What would you have me do in this situation?" As you consider your options, try to sense which one gives you the strongest feeling right of NEUTRAL towards g*odly* or being connected with God's will. After your *God check* is complete, go with His guidance.

During the experiment, you will at times feel influenced or tempted to make a choice that does not at all feel *godly*. Most likely it will be in those areas where you are most vulnerable to temptation. When this happens, assume (at least for the sake of the experiment) that *spiritual warfare* is at work attempting to keep you from being *online* to God. Assume an evil is at work, which celebrates in your failure and destruction. Remember, you don't have to believe this is true, I am only asking you to *assume* it is true.

With your inner voice say, "Not this time. God give me the strength to resist this temptation." You may end up with a real case of spiritual warfare on your hands. If you do, those things that are most tempting to you will likely be presented to you in the most tempting, compelling, perhaps even subtle, i.e., sneaky ways. You may even be tempted to say to yourself, "This is a stupid experiment. I don't believe in God anyway. I am going to do what I want."

"Which wolf will you feed?"

Please resist those thoughts. **You cannot seek God and consciously not do His will at the same time!** When yielding to God's will, try to rely on *love of God* rather than *fear of God*. Follow His will out of your love for Him and let His empowering love work *through* you. Each time you prevail in a round of spiritual warfare, you are coming closer to God. He'll seem more willing to strengthen His relationship with you and reveal more of Himself to you. He will keep His promise.

When you fail, as you will, please simply acknowledge your failure to God (or your assumption of God). Remember He is a forgiving God. Like a loving parent, He loves a repentant heart. Like a loving parent, His heart is broken when our decisions are self-destructive.

If you sincerely try to please God and stay *online* to God's power, you will make amazing progress. In fact, check your progress periodically, especially after prevailing in a round of spiritual warfare. You can *literally* or *mentally* use the following scale:

How connected or online do I feel to God now?

More _____ _____ _____ _____ _____ _____ _____ More
the last 1   2   3   4   5   6   7   this
Observation   Observation

A good way to routinely check your progress is to post this scale where you routinely see it, e.g., your bathroom mirror. If you are scoring four or higher on the scale, you are stable or are growing spiritually. If you are scoring less than four, your *online* connection might be weakening. Don't give up if that happens. It might just be neglect or lack of prayer time. It might be the result of losing a battle of spiritual warfare. Don't be discouraged; there are many battles. The goal is to win the war.

You might check your commitment effort. *Pray* – do a *God check* – are you striving for *godly* decisions? Are there problems with your lifestyle *you know* are not pleasing to God? Are you falling into the trap of saying to God, I will give up *this* for You but not *that*? Please trust me on this issue; you don't want to bargain with God. You want to *commit* to Him. That is how you get *online*.

Sometimes, I foolishly become discouraged when life isn't going the way I want it to. Being *online* with God does not eliminate life's problems, Matthew 5:45, *"He causes his sun to rise on the evil and the good, and sends rain on the righteous and the unrighteous."* Being *online* gives us grace to cope with *life's rain*.

Control Periods

No matter how committed you are to the experiment, you will *log off* from God at times. How do I know? Because we are human. Without intending to, you will create *offline* control periods to compare with your *online* treatment periods. You *log off* because you get distracted, lose focus or forget to stay *online*. You may simply make a few decisions using *your* will and resort to your old way of living *offline*. You are like a PC defaulting to *offline* when the *online* connection is not used for an extended period of time – you simply become disconnected. When you do, you lose access to God's wisdom for your decision making.

I have found that I can't *deliberately* commit a sin while *online* with God – with Him present in my conscious stream of thought. I have to *log off* – a definitive clue I am doing wrong. Just because I *log off* doesn't mean God doesn't know what wrong I have done. When I do this I am separating myself from the wonderful parental wisdom and love of God. The more I realize that, the more motivated I am to make decisions that keep me *online*. That's where there is peace and joy. Sin becomes easier to resist in a *supernatural* way.

God Raises the Bar – A Final Story

The more time I spend *online* with God, the more insight and wisdom He provides into what He expects and requires of one to be *online*. He continues to raise the bar as He helps me grow spiritually.

I could share many revealing, humbling growth experiences with you. But this chapter is already long enough, so I will share only one.

I wrote the first chapter of this book in the autumn of 2001, shortly after the events of **9/11**. I then got distracted with personal and professional matters. I kept thinking about getting back to this book, but

I didn't seem to have the time and didn't feel inspired. I began to doubt if it were a worthwhile project.

In September of 2002, I received an inheritance check for a substantial amount of money after the death of an uncle. His wife, my mother's sister, had already died. This aunt and uncle had no children; they left their estate to their nieces and nephews.

You may recall earlier in the book, I explained I was on my own at 19 and put myself though college. I was poor, lived in a small mobile home and sometimes had a tight food budget.

When I started realizing significant income, giving my fair share to God's work was a challenge for me. I was weak in my faith in God, but had faith in having *money in the bank*. When my faith was stronger, I gave more. But I was running a lifetime *giving to God* deficit.

I could always rationalize about not giving by considering *how much* I gave instead of how much I *should* give. I could always point to the misuse of money by the *suspect TV evangelists* that I described in **Chapter 2.**

Meanwhile, this inheritance check was staring at me. It is the only *easy money* that I had ever or likely would receive. I initially fantasized about self-indulgent expenditures. But my frugal nature kicked in, and I started looking for investments. The stock market bust of 2001, made stocks questionable, so I started investigating land investments. I began to take considerable time looking at properties. Suddenly, I realized I had put off working on this book because I didn't have time, but I was *burning up* time looking at real estate.

I realized I had not done an *online God check* concerning God's will for this money. When I did, He gently reminded me of my *giving to God* deficit. His guidance was to give all the money to God's work. I was sure I was *hallucinating;* I decided to give the decision a little more time. But my *online* time became consumed with God directing me to donate the inheritance.

This inheritance approximated my accumulative income for the first ten years I was married. To think of giving it up to God was troubling. (I am reluctantly obligated to mention, my wife had no problem giving the money to God.) But I was sure I would have second thoughts after the fact. I was in spiritual warfare between right and wrong. I had been there before, starting with my first spiritual experiment years ago. I decided to conduct a most expensive experiment. to give the inheritance to the Navigators, a non-denomination ministry for business and professional people. Rob Mahon is a navigator and a spiritual mentor with *God's fingerprints* all over him. Though he never asked for financial support, I knew his ministry had needs. I trusted he would make good use of *God's money.*

After I made the decision, but before I gave the inheritance, something amazing happened: Ideas for this book flooded my mind. I had authored many books before – but I had never experienced *being in the zone* as I was for this one. I worked days, nights and weekends. I wrote on airplanes and in hotel rooms. The explanation of difficult concepts became readily available to me when needed. As an author, I had never been inspired like this before; the first draft of this book was finished in a few short weeks.

While I was writing the book, God revealed two significant things to me about the temptation of that inheritance money. First, He didn't need it. I *needed* to be *able* to give it. Giving it brought me closer to God, allowing me to finish this book. That wisdom is documented in the Bible, *"For where your treasure is, there your heart will be also,"* (Matthew 6:21). Writing this book was a profound spiritual experience.

The second revelation is a real eye-opener. Do you remember in **Chapter 2** how thoroughly I *judged* the TV evangelists for using God's money in self-indulgent ways? Through my inner voice, God said to me, "Jim, when you don't give to God what you should, you are keeping what is God's. If you spend God's money on yourself, how are you any different than the TV evangelists who misuse resources dedicated to God?" That wisdom is of course in the Bible too, "*For in the same way you judge others, you will be judged...,*" (Matthew 7:2).

What was special about the way God *spoke* to me through my inner voice was that it was not harsh or judgmental. It was gentle, like a loving parent seizing a *teachable moment*, a moment of enlightenment that brought me closer to God. He had *raised the bar* when He thought I was able to understand his message, to remind me that I am *work in progress*. Perhaps life is an *experiential experiment* that allows us to work, test and prepare ourselves for eternal life.

CONCLUSION

I hope the spiritual experiment discussed above is meaningful to your relationship with God. You may have noticed that during this chapter I did not present the alternative that God might not exist. I assumed if you didn't believe, at least a little, you would have abandoned the book long before now. If you are still struggling, it is okay. You are still seeking. Be patient. God has His reasons.

If your faith is strengthened by this book, that is wonderful. The book has served its purpose. But don't stop seeking to know Him in deeper ways. Please continue to assess your *online* connection to God and strengthen it. Some ways to do that are provided in the next and last chapter. The more connected you are, the more He reveals His wonder to you.

I continue to have questions and issues with God. In the final chapter, I share some of what God has revealed in response to some of those needs. These answers are the result of Bible study, attending church, meaningful discussions with *godly* people and spending time *online* with God. Specifically, I will share thoughts on:

- ❖ How much time God can give you

- ❖ 'Lying' as the pivotal sin

- ❖ Why faith doesn't need to be intellectual

- ❖ Bible interpretation

- ❖ Perspectives on Jesus Christ

- ❖ Giving vs. taking

CHAPTER 6

EPIPHANIES FROM PRAYER –
DOWNLOADS FROM GOD

This chapter is intended to be *icing on the cake* if the previous five chapters were helpful. As my faith grows, so does my understanding of wisdom, wonder and God accessibility.

I encourage students to always ask questions when they don't understand. As a *God-student*, I go to Him in prayer and ask for answers to troubling questions, and in His time, when He feels I am ready, He answers.

Most of what is written in this book is based upon answers or epiphanies to prayerful inquiries. These epiphanies – moments of sudden understanding – occur at any time. They often wake me. Suddenly an answer to a question such as, "Why is there death?" or "Why can't we understand more about God?" stirs me awake. I keep bedside paper and pens to record my inner voice when it speaks, and these tend to be enlightening, joyful, spiritual moments.

Please don't think I consider my understanding of these moments to be 100 percent accurate. As a human, my interpretations undoubtedly fall short of the mark. Like students solving math problems, not all answers will be correct but some are closer than others. The closer to correct our interpretation of God's messages, the more useful and illuminating they are.

These moments of enlightenment are much more frequent and meaningful when I spend time with *godly* people and in Bible study, prayer and church. I also find it important to validate insights with Bible investigations and discussions with other *believers* and – believe it or not – *non-believers* who rigorously challenge my beliefs.

Some epiphanies are not the result of a prayerful question; they seem to come from *nowhere,* yet are startlingly relevant to my spiritual growth. For example, it was an epiphany when God enlightened me of my hypocrisy pertaining to TV evangelists as discussed at the end of **Chapter 5.** I'm not smart enough to ask for enlightenment in all areas needed: God must clue me in to them.

In the remainder of this chapter, I share some of the most helpful epiphanies God has provided either in answer to prayer or because He knew I had a need. Some epiphanies are short and to the point; others, like epiphany five, *Interpretation of the Bible,* and epiphany six, *Perspective on Jesus Christ,* require more explanation.

EPIPHANY ONE

God is Infinite; You can be Online Constantly

In my weaker faith days, I would attend church, going through the seeking-God *motions,* and though useful, these times were also *insufficient.* A good Sunday message would inspire me to behave in a more *godly* manner throughout the rest of the week. Even though I had my God doubts, there was value in aspiring to be a better, more moral person. But the *message* would usually *wear off* as the week went on and by the next Sunday, I needed more *spiritual inspiration.*

If I missed church for several weeks, I slipped out of the routine. Then I would go into *spiritual limbo* and make less *godly* decisions; there were times when I didn't attend church for months.

Intermittent Prayer Schedule

I generally prayed intermittently when I felt the need – or *had a need*. However when more spiritual, I'd pray daily. The book, **The Prayer of Jabez** (Multnomah, 2000), is an illustration of the usefulness of a daily prayer while providing a pray template, and daily prayer did make me feel more God-connected.

When I began the *spiritual experiment* described in **Chapter 5**, I would pray anytime I was tempted in my weak areas, and this was a significant adjustment. Usually when I faced temptation, e.g., losing my temper, a God thought was a last thought, and I was totally *offline* if I yielded to temptation.

Through the spiritual experiment, I began to overcome temptation and my *ungodly* impulses, and God began to reveal Himself to me in convincing ways. As I grew spiritually, God enlightened me with the *Internet metaphor* described in **Chapter 1**. I began to wonder about the extent I should be *online* with God and which decisions are worthy of His time.

Continuous Prayer with God Online

The *answer?* He has *infinite* capacity: There is *no decision* too small to seek His guidance. Like the Internet, He can expand to demand; I now try to have God *online* in my *consciousness stream* as much as possible. He has become my companion and counselor through my *inner voice*.

As an example, I frequent a cafeteria where many retired people also eat lunch. Sunday is the cafeteria's big business day – post-church. The managers say it's the staff's most *dreaded* day. Not because of increased workload, but because the after-church crowd is cranky. The staff's common joke, "These people must not have listened to the preacher today!"

One day I headed to the cafeteria to grab a quick lunch during a break from work on this book. As I came in the door, three 80-year-olds, one with an oxygen tank in-tow, were walking toward the food trays. I thought, "They will take *forever*." Just then they took the *long way* to the tray destination. This was my lucky break: I made a quick cut and beat the competition to the trays by 40 feet.

Priority Interrupt from God

As I started to feel clever and efficient, I reconnected to God, and my inner voice said, "Nice move, you just flaunted your good health and out-smarted a group of older patrons; undoubtedly they see the grace of God in you." My *human nature* stuck out like a sore thumb. I quickly prayed, "God that was stupid and selfish. I am sorry. Please give me guidance to overcome what I just did."

Upon completing my brief *God-check*, a quick solution came. I grabbed three trays and placed napkins and silverware on each. By the time the patrons I had *cut off at the pass* arrived, their trays were ready and waiting for them. They offered gentle, appreciative smiles and said, "How thoughtful of you." With God's guidance, I made *lemon-ade* out of my *behavioral lemon*.

Life is consecutive decision-making; God can guide you in each one – big *and* small.

EPIPHANY TWO

Love without Forgiveness is Cheap, Love with Forgiveness is Priceless

It's not challenging to love someone who always pleases you: Love is easily *abandoned* when someone you love *fails,* or worse – *betrays* you.

In studying Jesus' life I find it amazing that although *He never needed forgiveness, He forgave supernaturally.* I often struggle with forgiving *even* when someone apologizes for a failure or small betrayal. Jesus forgave to perfection – He forgave when there were no apologies even when He was wrongfully crucified (Luke 23:34).

Forgiveness is something all humans need. Whatever reasonable *code of conduct* you and I might agree to, e.g., the Ten Commandments, neither one of us is able to live up to it. We fail; forgiveness is mandatory. Without arguing the divinity of Jesus, we can learn much from His forgiving nature.

Fortunately for my daughter Jessie – and even more fortunate for me – I was *online* when we both required forgiving love. I had just picked up a new sports car that had been on order for more than a year. When I drove up to our house Jessie, who was 16, was there. She asked for a ride and wanted to drive the *new wheels*; I obliged. We came home, she parked the car in our driveway, and we went inside.

Five minutes later Jessie came screaming and crying into the house: She had *backed* her Jeep into my hour-old sports car. (It gets worse.) Only three months earlier she had backed into a different car, rented by a colleague, *parked in the same place.*

I'd never heard in her voice or seen in her eyes such fear and sorrow as she cried out the disparaging news. My heart sank when I realized what had happened. I thought to myself, "How could she be so careless?" Jessie is a brilliant, beautiful woman. She is a straight-A student, top one percent of her class: Her academic performance far exceeds my own. But like me, her mind can get preoccupied; she doesn't always pay attention.

I quickly got *online* with God and prayed, "Please give me grace." He did. My focus shifted from my damaged car to not damaging my relationship with my precious child. I know what it feels like to be *so sorry you can't bear it*, at those times forgiveness is the *world* to the transgressor.

Had I responded with my *offline* humanism, my response could've caused irreparable damage: Children outweigh possessions.

Later I thanked God for the *grace-grant*. As I grew spiritually, I realized the car smash was a blessing: How often do you get a chance to express your love through memorable forgiveness? An opportunity to forgive is an opportunity to show your love is *unconditional* – an opportunity to show God at work.

My non-Christian friends often tell me the dynamic they find particularly appealing about Christianity is the strong emphasis on forgiveness. *Me too.*

EPIPHANY THREE

If You Commit Not to Lie, Sinning Becomes More Difficult

Whether you view the Adam and Eve story as literal or metaphorical, did you notice the first documented failing of humanity is caused by lying (Genesis 3:4 – "*You will not surely die*," the serpent said to the woman)? Lying is a *cornerstone* for other sins. If you make a *decision not to lie*, it makes it increasingly difficult to commit other sins. Most other sins sooner or later require a concealing lie – as was the case for Adam and Eve.

A major advantage of the truth – it's *easier* to remember. Accordingly, when recalling past events you just have to remember reality. When we spin lies, we have to remember twists and the truths. I know someone who spent his career as an IRS criminal investigator, arresting many drug dealers via tax fraud. A useful tactic of his was getting suspects to repeatedly run through the 'facts.' When they lied, they just couldn't keep a story straight because they couldn't remember prior *versions*: They'd get stuck in lies.

White Lies Lead to Destructive Lies

Lying is subtle sin because it often begins with the ever-seductive *white lie* – told in an attempt to be nice. We might not tell someone the truth to avoid hurting feelings, but telling *white lies* is a short step to more destructive lies.

I Remember the First Lie I Told My Wife

In most marriages, it seems the husband has the stronger sex drive, especially after children are born. This desire difference can cause marital friction. According to a recent study, the *two most* common fights in marriage are *money* and *sex* – not always in that order.

The Act of Marriage: the Beauty of Sexual Love (Zondervan, revised 1998) by Tim and Beverly La Haye is a book that I wish my wife and I had read when we wed. It explains male vs. female psychology of sex, the physical vs. the emotional, respectively. (And then there's the pesky imbalance of desire for sexual frequency.)

At any rate, about a year into our marriage my wife asked, "Do you ever think about other women in a sexual way?" As a man and *physical* being, I was afraid she'd only understand the white lie men often tell: "Of course not!"

I wish I'd told the truth and said, "Sometimes I do look at women in a physical way, but you are the woman I love. Making love with *you* is important to me. It's a strong need that must be fulfilled for my happiness. What is important to you emotionally, so I can be responsive to your needs?"

The truth would have provided my wife a better understanding of me and motivated her to please me, as I wanted to please her. Perhaps because I lied, we didn't uncover our need differences for many years and consequently, sex found a place in our *top-hit-list* of *fusses*.

Lies to hide sin are usually more destructive than truth, and lying is such a futile sin. You might fool others but *never* God. Consequently, you are bound to tell the truth – unless you tell yourself He doesn't exist, but then there's no God *online*.

EPIPHANY FOUR

It Wouldn't be Fair if Faith had to be Intellectual

But accepting God doesn't seem *reasonable*. This is especially an issue for academicians and the mentally endowed. They boast, "How can intelligent, well-educated, independent people invest in the nonsensical?" To support this case, they point to *less-educated* believers as evidence that faith is not for intellectuals.

An argument easily derailed with one question, "How could a *fair* God be accessible *only* if you're smart?"

Satan manipulates the *intelligent* in a *simple* fashion. Submitting to God is more challenging for those with *delusions of grandeur*. Paradoxically, the only crime Jesus was accused of was blasphemy, yet His humility is well-documented.

Whatever *natural* aptitude we get is a gift – not earned. Proverbs 11:2 says, "*When pride comes, then comes disgrace, but with humility comes wisdom.*"

EPIPHANY FIVE

Bible Interpretation – You Can Take the Wisdom Literally

In **Chapter 5,** using the Bible as a reference, I argued that you could *seek* and *find* God without Bible access. The cornerstone argument: a *fair* God wouldn't penalize a *seeker* because he or she couldn't access a Bible. If you accepted that reasoning, would it not follow you can have an ongoing relationship with God without the Bible?

However, if you do have access to religious resources, including the Bible, how should they *affect* your relationship to God? If they're from God, should they not *enrich* it? This brings us to the controversial issue of Bible interpretation. Is the Bible the *word* of God, *inspired* by God or humans' *understanding* of God? Some argue for nothing less than a *literal* interpretation of the entire Bible: an interesting position given that there are times Jesus speaks *figuratively*.

For example, in Mark 9:43-47, Jesus tells us to amputate hands/feet or pluck out eyes which cause our sins – no Bible study guide says to take that *literally*. In Luke 13:32, Jesus refers to Herod as a *fox* – clearly figurative language. Is it possible to decipher the Bible *literally-figuratively*? Or should we accept the Bible uses normal language containing *figurative* and *literal* expressions, as do we when we communicate?

Another example, hell is described as a place of fire and darkness. Wouldn't flames light things up? This seems to be figurative language providing meaningful imagery for the indescribable. Hell is about separation from God for those who refuse to accept Him – a conscious *decision*. We live in a world that has free choice; however God is still involved. I believe this is why the truly evil never prevail; even Hitler crumbled. Can you imagine an existence without God's influence and those who love God removed? This is difficult to convey without resorting to figurative scenarios.

Some argue that just certain Bible segments should be taken literally, e.g., the Ten Commandments, the Beatitudes – Jesus' Sermon on the Mount. No matter what portion of the Bible is taken literally, I've often noticed these debaters have never truly studied the Bible, and the only worthwhile debates are among the Bible knowledgeable. People often attribute and argue non-Biblical statements as Biblical, e.g., "God works in mysterious ways."

Nonetheless, before we concern ourselves with *literal* or *non-literal* positions, let's see what basics we can learn about interpretation through logical and empirical evaluation.

Communication Problems in General

We know the Bible is communication – specifically written communication. What do we know about communication in general from personal experience? We know words are our primary tools (we also use body language, voice inflection, gestures, expressions, etc.). What do we know about words? They're thought translations and as such have limitations, e.g., my feeling of love for my family is difficult to *word*.

The challenge with communication is as follows: I have a thought or image in my mind that I *translate* into words. You read the words and make your own interpretation based upon your experience and understanding of the words. Generally, something is lost in translation.

With verbal communication we have the advantage of asking for clarification. This is a tremendous aid. We can exchange information until we achieve understanding, but that aid is lost in written communication unless we have access to the author.

Book as an Illustration

To illustrate the challenge of written communication, please consider this book. As I write this book, I will think for a while and then try to express a thought's essence into words. Then I reread and revise until I think I have expressed my thoughts as well as I can.

My wife of 34 years usually reads the first draft. She knows me better than anyone else on the planet, but I'm often dismayed at how she misunderstands my written *expression of thought*.

I make revisions based on her comments, and we repeat this review process until she understands in *her way* what I am trying to say, i.e., she interprets *my words* into *her thoughts*. I repeat these revisions with others of different ages, backgrounds and beliefs. Based on their feedback, often indicating I failed to communicate effectively to varying audiences, I revise the words.

Nevertheless, no matter how hard I try, people will understandably interpret what I mean in an unintended way. A major problem is that the same words mean *different* things to *different* people. For example, what is the meaning of *too expensive*? To college students, to CEOs, to someone who forgot his wallet? Independent of the *range* of what constitutes expensive are *affordability, fairness* and *willingness*. By *too expensive* I might mean:

1. The price is fine, but I can't afford it.
2. I can afford it, but the price is not fair.
3. I can afford it and the price is fair, but I'm unwilling to spend that much.

All three conditions are expressed identically; without clarification we can talk about *different* issues using the *same* words – *too expensive*.

Contracts as Illustration

Another illustration of word limitation is a typical contract. A contract's purpose is to assure a *meeting of minds* as to what has been *agreed* upon. In an attempt to eliminate *misunderstanding*, contracts tend to be elaborately wordy. So wordy, most people need an attorney to *translate*.

Context Changes Everything

As if there aren't enough word problems, let's examine the impact of *context*. There are five pertinent context issues: *intended audience, language translation, cultural mores/norms, passage of time* and *socio-economic factors*.

As an author and speaker I have had to adjust my message according to the audience. Speeches for executives differ than those for students, and with international audiences, translators occasionally can't find words equivalent to what I'm trying to say.

The *language translation* is particularly challenging when spiritual material is translated from its original tongue as with the Koran. When translated from Arabic to English, westerners complain about readability and Muslims say the linguistic beauty meaningful for recitation, is lost. Catholics share this criticism when Mass is conducted in English rather than Latin.

Passage of time is a sensitive issue: I discussed earlier the inadequacy of the word *love*, especially when trying to describe marital/child relations over time. Even consider how *Web* and *Net* have gone from *spiders* and *fishing* to *computer network terminology* since the 1990s. Consider how the term *rich man* has changed since Biblical times: *Socio-economically* speaking, a rich man from Biblical times is comparable to middle class Americans. And in Biblical times, groups were without social mobility, i.e., once a slave, always a slave and no government interventions.

Historical Review of the Bible

Before we focus on Bible interpretation, let's get a historical perspective. First, what is the Bible? It is concurrently viewed throughout the world as literature, history and Holy Scripture. Some view it as one of the three, others as two of three and others as all of the above. The Hebrew Bible, referred to by some Christians as the Old Testament, is a collection of books compiled over a 1,400-year period ending about 400 B.C. It was most likely assembled into its current Books of Law, Prophets and Writings about 300 B.C., making it a historical and religious book to Jewish people and revered in much of the New Testament and Koran.

The New Testament was written during the first century A.D., mainly consisting of instructional letters to early Christians. First century Christians began selecting and organizing these letters/books into volumes, including the Hebrew Bible because Christianity's roots are in Judaism. There are more than 220 quotes of Old Testament passages disbursed throughout the New Testament and more than 100 quotes from Jesus alone, as well as Old Testament prophecies mentioned and fulfilled in the New Testament. The final organization of the New Testament and the Christian Bible occurred sometime in the fourth century.

The Christian Bible was written during a span of 1,500 years, by more than 40 Jewish authors (except for Luke who was likely Greek), in three different languages and contains more than 31,000 verses. If you read an English version of the Bible, translations from Hebrew, Greek and Aramaic were necessary.

Perspectives on the Koran, Dharma, and Scriptures of Hinduism

Though this book explores interpretation of the Bible, perspectives on the writings of other religions are useful and meaningful. First, the Koran was written by the prophet Mohammed through revelations he received during a 23-year period beginning in 610 A.D. In *A History of God* (Ballentine, 1994), Karen Armstrong explains that to Muslims the Koran is the spiritual equivalent of what Jesus' teachings are to Christians. Mohammed believed that Al-Lah was the same God worshipped by Jews and Christians, and he viewed the Koran as an extension of the Bible, and indeed many teachings are similar. The Koran refers to prophets like Abraham, Moses and Jesus (Koran 2:135-136) without teaching/accepting the deity of Christ.

Asia's dominant religion, Buddhism, was founded in 500 B.C. when Buddha (Siddhartha Gautama) sought spiritual enlightenment after becoming disillusioned with the unhappiness and suffering of life and left his wealthy, powerful royal family – including his wife and infant son. The Dharma is a collection of this wandering monk's teachings, instructing that existence is a continuous death, rebirth cycle. People are reincarnated at different levels of well-being based on behavioral *goodness* during previous lives. This cycle can be broken by detachment from worldly desires/materials, allowing people to achieve perfect peace and happiness, or *nirvana*.

Hinduism, India's dominant religion, is polytheistic, i.e., the belief in multiple gods. However, many Hindus believe gods/divinities compose one universal spirit, Brahman. As the oldest living religion, Hinduism has no single book like the Bible, the Koran or the Dharma but instead has sacred writings, including the Vedas, Puranas, Ramayana, Mahabharata, Bhagavad-Gita and Manu Smriti, which teach reincarnation where souls are reborn as either animals or persons. Hinduism also teaches the law of karma, i.e., all human action influences how a soul returns in the next incarnation. As in Buddhism, this rebirth cycle continues until a soul achieves spiritual perfection; at this time the soul enters a new level of existence, *moksha*, and never returns to earth.

Both Buddhism and Hinduism embrace goodness/morality and spirituality as crucial goals without embracing a monolithic God.

Reincarnation is a significant obstacle to the experimental/logical approach used for faith in this book. I have no experiential recollection of any previous life – near death research stretches me far enough. Accordingly, using the *know-what-I-know-and-don't-know* tools leave me skeptical of reincarnation.

Bible Interpretation

Because of communication issues discussed earlier, even a literal Biblical translation breeds interpretation challenges. There can even be different understandings of the exact same scripture. For example, the Bible says that a leader in the church should have only one wife (1 Timothy 3:12). Does "one wife" mean "one wife at a time", i.e., no polygamy; however remarriage is allowed through death or divorce? Or does it mean "one wife in a lifetime"? David, Solomon and others had many wives (2 Samuel 3:2-5 and 1 Kings 11:3) and there are provisions for multiple wives in the Bible (Deuteronomy 21:15 and 25:5) and for divorce (Deuteronomy 24:1-3 and Matthew 5:31). What's the literal explanation for rules and the practice of polygamy in the Bible?

This is one of many perplexing Biblical issues. Many experts say that God never approved of polygamy, e.g., Deuteronomy 17:17; but He tolerated it and provided laws to govern it. I've yet to find a Biblical scholar/study guide resolving multiple wives; as such, it remains one of my *backburner* issues. For me, much of the Bible's beauty rests in continually delving into answer adventures in the text and/or company of others.

The point: Bible interpretation latitude ranges, i.e., the advice of contrary scholars and study guides. I do believe God inspired the Bible's authors, i.e., Mark 10:5. Jesus speaking on divorce says, "*It was because your hearts were hard that Moses wrote you this law.*" Notice that Jesus didn't say *God told Moses* to write the law – though many interpret that as a given.

I'm an academic author attempting to write a spiritual book. I know it's not God's literal word otherwise I wouldn't need revisions. At times I do feel *inspired* and have had *spiritual moments* when writing solutions come via prayer. I've made a *sincere* effort to communicate truth, as *purely* as I understand it, and I don't doubt people will *read* my words differently (I hope better) than intended.

Where does this Leave Us?

In my early 30s, I rigorously studied the Bible cover to cover using extensive study guides to convince myself of God's existence, and I became bewildered. Much of the Bible is God's covenants/contracts with His people; the challenge of contractual communication (and attorneys) is discussed earlier. What I couldn't understand on my own, e.g., multiple wives, I pursued with Bible experts, and their answers or candid answer-less admissions discouraged me and resulted in *spiritual limbo.*

Post a few *piano droppings*, I finally started praying in the manner discussed in **Chapter 5**, i.e., spiritual experiment, and via the *experiment* I began **experiencing God**. Once I relied on His promise to seekers and abided by my God consciousness, He became real – I was *online.* I tried finding God through *intellectual* efforts and *failed.* When I tried to find Him through *spiritually* assisted efforts I *succeeded.* Now I have a *humble intellectual* appreciation of God and His wisdom, and as I grow in faith, that *online* connection increases in strength/bandwidth.

Mark Twain, a self-proclaimed atheist, indicated that it wasn't what he didn't understand about the Bible that troubled him, it was what he did. I work at both, accepting that because of intended audience, language translation, cultural mores, time passage, and socio-economic issues and use of figurative language, interpretation is further complicated. But I do take literally the **wisdom** I find in the Bible, i.e., the consequences of *godly* and *ungodly* behavior, to guide my decision-making processes.

The Bible offers documentation of God's will. When we choose we can seek guidance via the Bible *and* from God *online* efforts. When they converge, we have confidence in the correctness of decisions. In situations without this convergence, I seek *replication* of a *godly* feeling (right of NEUTRAL) or counsel from *godly* people I trust. And when God's will isn't textually expressed in the Bible, the *spirit* often is and can be sought/confirmed via these other means.

Final thought

When we make decisions, our goal should be to receive the full benefit of God's wisdom from Him, through the Bible and fellow believers. With freedom of choice to explore these three outlets, God gives us the advantage of multiple wisdom outlets to consciously increase our *online* connection with the knowledge that the more we seek, the more we find.

EPIPHANY SIX

Perspective on Jesus Christ

Who is Jesus Christ? In my interpretation, that is the most significant, fundamental difference among the Hebrew Bible, the Koran and the Christian Bible. What is Jesus' relationship to the God of Abraham who is accepted by all three religions? As indicated in **Chapter 1,** I am a Christian, and this is an important admission before I discuss my Christ reasoning.

Christian Defined

First, I should define what I mean by 'Christian,' as interpretation of this word varies. For example, Christian refers to a number of religious denominations. And while in Israel, I learned Christians were more a political party than a faith because of the slight separation of government and religion, i.e., Israel is referred to as a Jewish country, Saudi Arabia as Muslim and Ireland as Christian, although there is a contentious relationship between Catholics and Protestants that appears to have little to do with faith in God. As for my Christian definition, I use the *Holman Bible Dictionary* (Holman, 1991):

> *A Christian is an adherent to Christ; one committed to Christ; a follower of Christ. The word is used three times in the New Testament. **1.** Believers "were called Christians first in Antioch" because their behavior, activity, and speech were like Christ (Acts 11:26). **2.** Agrippa responded to Paul's witness, "Almost thou persuade me to be a Christian" (Acts 26:28). He spoke of becoming an adherent of Christ. **3.** Peter stated that believers who "suffer as a Christian" are to do so for the glory of God (1 Peter 4:16). A **Christian is one who becomes an adherent of Christ, whose daily life and behavior in facing adversity is like Christ.***

Impact of Christ

Why place so much emphasis on Christ? When we discussed research in **Chapter 3**, we debated the need to avoid the *causality trap*, and considerations of *alternative* explanations for empirical outcomes became a key technique in trap avoidance. If we use a *historical research* approach pondering the *treatment* effect of Jesus' teachings, we gain insightful perspective, graphically depicted as follows:

```
                            Treatment
Undated--- - - - - ? - - - - ---Jesus' Ministry---------Present
Creation              Crucifixion & Ascension
                          26/27 to 30 A.D.
```

Note that so profound were the *before-and-after* effects of Christ's life that even the world calendar reflects His influence: Before Christ (B.C.) and after Christ, i.e., anno Domini, (A.D.).   The worldly effects of Christianity, i.e., apostles/disciples writings, divisions of Christian worship, churches and every *Christian* act/life throughout history can be traced to a three to four-year *treatment* period approximately 2000 years ago.

Not every effect traceable to the lessons of Christ is positive, e.g., the Christian Crusades, Inquisition, false prophets, deceptive TV evangelists.   However, those actions are not based on Christ's *teachings:* History swells with religious *hijackers* using *teachings* for evil and oppressive purposes, e.g., terrorists and/or religious fundamentalists. With these hijackings, incorrect conclusions about religious teachings often occur.   To avoid this, it's crucial to frequent the most *authentic/original source* of all religious teachings to seek correct understanding.

The teachings of Mohammed, Buddha and the scriptures of Hinduism also have significant 'treatment' effects – good and sometimes bad – on the world. Accordingly, seeking understanding of God is enriched by exploring how others *build their bridge to their faith.* Are we not all influenced/limited by what we are taught and our access to religious materials? Shouldn't a *responsible seeker* challenge his or her beliefs by contrasting them against others? If God wants us to seek, does He not reward heartfelt, sincere seeking with revealing insight? But should we not also accept that given the limits of *relative intelligence* humans are not likely to achieve either consensus or perfect *divine insight?*

Go to the Source

We have the benefit of accessing the teachings of Jesus. The New Testament is the best resource to understand Jesus and His word. Keep in mind the original message was spoken primarily in Hebrew or Aramaic and recorded several decades later by Matthew, Mark, Luke and John (N = 4 sample size). And though complementary, the historical accounts of Jesus' life and ministry aren't identical, e.g., Matthew and Mark mention Jesus traveling to Jerusalem once, while John has Jesus in Jerusalem several times.

A convenient way to study Jesus' instruction is to use a *red-letter* Bible edition where all quotes attributed to Jesus are printed in red letters; check out the Beatitudes or Jesus' Sermon on the Mount. Two separate but complementary accounts are provided in Matthew 5-7 and Luke 6:17-26. Important point: Jesus is an unpublished teacher – others documented His spoken word.

Christ's teachings called into question the reality of His time: He taught *heartfelt obedience* outweighs *legalistic observance* of God's *rules*. Armed with this idea, He propelled a global intervention – Christianity – for which there is no *alternative* explanation.

What is Jesus' Relationship to God?

Most people, Jews/Muslims included, accept Jesus as a moral teacher, perhaps even a prophet, but controversy looms around whether or not He was the Messiah, the Son of God or God incarnate – part of a divine trinity including God, the Father and the Holy Spirit.

Studying words attributed to Jesus in the New Testament doesn't completely clarify this issue, and the Bible never mentions the divine trinity concept. Jesus does proclaim to be the Messiah (Luke 4:17-21, John 4:25-26), while others refer to Him as Son of Man and Son of God. Jesus acknowledges He is both (Matthew 26:64, Mark 14:62, Luke 22: 68-70).

There are also times Jesus indicates God and the Holy Spirit are separate entities from Himself (Matthew 6:9, 12:32,50, 18:35, 19:4, Luke 9:48, 11:13, John 20:21-22). John is the only author who records

Jesus stating He and God are One (John 10:30). However in the same paragraph, Jesus speaks of performing miracles in His Father's name (John 10:25).

The Jesus/God relationship is difficult to decipher with the limitations of relative intelligence (as discussed in **Chapter 5**). From all accounts, Jesus lived an extraordinary, sinless life, and His teachings are world altering. But is Jesus deity – God incarnate?

Given this book's approach on how we *know what we know*, we are left with theories/interpretations that can be *experientially* used to seek God and His mystery. The documentation of Jesus' life shows He was *God online* beyond anything observed in (other) humans. As for deity, I believe a supernatural relationship existed between Jesus and God, but I don't expect understanding in this life. **Deity** and **divine trinity** are similar to **infinity** and **eternity**: beyond the reach of my limited *relative intelligence*. This doesn't trouble me; I'm fascinated that in another life I will understand.

Compelling Evidence

The Bible documents Jesus' mission commitment was such that He predicted and endured crucifixion followed by resurrection – assuming the Biblical accounts of Matthew, Mark, Luke and John are accurate. Most of the apostles suffered a martyr's death for gospel spreading, according to the ***Holman Bible Dictionary*** (Holman Bible Publishers, 1991). Why would they risk death for something they didn't *know* to be true?

Of the apostles who died a martyr's death, Peter's story is especially enlightening. To avoid persecution Peter denied knowing Jesus three times the night before Jesus' crucifixion – just as Jesus said he would (Matthew 26:69-75, Mark 14:66-72, Luke 22:57-60, John 18:17,25-27). But after Christ's *alleged* resurrection, Peter spoke of the teachings, crucifixion and resurrection, while fully aware it would likely result in a martyr's crucifixion. He had plenty of warning: The Sanhedrin jailed Peter (Acts 4:3), Herod seized Peter, but he escaped (Act 12:2-11).

Eventually, Peter seems to have died a martyr in Rome in the 60s A.D. – quite a turnabout from a man who thrice denied Christ. Could a possible explanation of Peter's behavior be that he saw a resurrected Christ?

Final Thoughts

Jesus reassures us of a key promise: *"For everyone who asks receives; he who seeks finds; and to him who knocks, the door will be opened"* (Matthew 7:8). If the spiritual experiment of **Chapter 5** works in your life, you have empirical evidence, and that experience can be *externally validated* via Bible study and interactions with *godly* people.

When Jesus was asked to name the greatest commandment, He said: *"Love the Lord your God with all your heart and with all your soul and with all your mind. This is the first and greatest commandment. And the second is like it: Love your neighbor as yourself. All the Laws and the Prophets hang on these two commandments"* (Matthew 22:37-40; also see Mark 12:30-31).

If we all did as *Jesus taught*, would the world be a better place? The closest glimpse of this world is derived from *exceptional believers* discussed in **Chapter 2**. They are the Christians who conform to Christ's image in a compelling way, embodying *empirical* evidence and *validating* Christ's teaching.

❖ No matter what *status* they achieve, they have a *serving attitude*.

❖ No matter what *adversities* they face, they are *faithful and joyful*.

❖ No matter their level of *success,* they are *generous, grateful* and *humble.*

❖ No matter if dealing with *fools,* they respond with *patience* and *wisdom.*

❖ No matter the temptation to be *judgmental,* they influence those who sin through *kindness* and *example.*

❖ No matter if *treated wrongfully,* they respond with *forgiving grace.*

❖ No matter when they fail as humans, they respond with *contrition.*

The *Christ-like behavior* of these believers *persuades* me to be a Christian.

In Philippians 2:5-9, Paul wrote: *"Your attitude should be the same as that of Christ Jesus: Who, being in very nature God, did not consider equality with God something to be grasped, but made himself nothing, taking the very nature of a servant, being made in human likeness. And being found in appearance as a man, he humbled himself and became obedient to death – even death on a cross! Therefore God exalted him to the highest place and gave him the name that is above every name."*

Unlike what I experience with *intellectuals* who have an ego-based *God-complex,* Christ presented absolute humility.

EPIPHANY SEVEN

Giving is for Our Benefit

Jesus said, *"It is more blessed to give than to receive,"* (Acts 20:35). In my *spiritual limbo* days, this seemed like a hustler's line. I used to think, "Yeah right!" Because of my self-sufficient secular skills, I *seldom* needed others. I was usually on the *giving* side of most relationships. Though most people were grateful, I was often surprised at the lack of gratitude shown.

My first glimpse – or epiphany – into how God must view our generosity came from my daughter Jamie when she was six years old. One Easter she was celebrating finding her basket of goodies, enthusiastically rummaging through treats we prepared for her.

Suddenly Jamie stopped, selected one of the better chocolates and brought it to me, "Here Daddy, I want you to have this one."

It was one of my most treasured gifts because I didn't *need* or *want* a chocolate, especially since *weight management* had become an issue. The *wonderful* came from the *goodness* and *giving spirit* within her to share with her father. Of course I didn't eat the chocolate; it became a treasure I kept in my desk drawer – a reminder of a special moment.

I realized when we give as God asks, it's not to fulfill any need He has. Rather, He's developing *giving spirits* bringing us closer to Him – making us more like Christ, allowing us to experience unexpected joy.

I shared with you how giving the piano to the church and giving the inheritance to the Navigators were blessings in unusual and meaningful ways for me: God taught me His word is true – *it is more blessed to give than to receive.*

CONCLUSION

As one closing example, I share with you the experience of writing this book. You will recall in the opening of **Chapter 1**, I promised God if I could ever achieve faith that I would serve him. Of course I never *achieved* faith, it was God's gift-in-waiting to be *received* only when I was ready. Having received rather than achieved faith, I was even more motivated to honor my commitment.

Writing this book was part of that commitment, a humble gift to God and you. The more I give to God, however, the more He blesses me in return. The act of writing this book forced a spiritual quake allowing my faith, love, closeness to and understanding of God to grow exponentially. And I pray it serves you.

If this book helped in your God quest, and if you are not already doing so, please find a place of worship and education that enriches your *God online* connection.

Seeking is a magnificent lifetime journey. God is not an *omnipotent dictator* who forces His presence and will upon us. Rather, He gives us God 'consciousness' and the *opportunity* to seek Him. If we *choose* to respond to this opportunity, He reveals Himself in convincing ways rendering life *offline* as shallow and trivial compared to **God online**. This book began with the following four questions:

1. What is life's meaning?
2. Is there a God?
3. Is there life after death?
4. How can I have peace and contentment?

My sincere hope is that the approach shared in this book has been helpful to *your* answers to these questions.

My answers? I believe that the meaning of life is to connect to God and learn the true meaning of love and forgiveness. Through this learning we find peace and contentment and prepare ourselves for life beyond this one.

With warmest regards,

James C. Wetherbe

P.S. C U *Online*

SELECTED REFERENCES

Armstrong, Karen. *A History of God*, New York: Ballentine, 1994

Armstrong, Karen. *The Battle for God*, New York: Ballantine, 2001.

Blackmore, Susan. *Dying to Live: Near Death-Experiences*, Buffalo: Prometheus, 1993.

Brinkley, Dannion, Paul Perry and Raymond A. Moody. *Saved by the Light*, San Francisco: Harper, 1995.

Campbell, Donald T. and Julian C. Stanley. *Experimental and Quasi-Experimental Designs for Research*, Boston: Houghton Mifflin, 1966.

Collins, James and Jerry Porras. *Built to Last: Successful Habits of Visionary Companies*, New York: Harper Business, 1994.

Cook, Thomas D., Donald T. Campbell and Thomas H. Cook. *Quasi-Experimentation: Design and Analysis Issues*, Boston: Houghton Mifflin, 1979.

Croswhite, Steele. *"The Way", Stand*, Minneapolis: Redline, 2002.

Davis, Duane. *Business Research for Decision Making*, Duxbury Press, 1999.

Dukes, W. "N=1," *Psychological Bulletin*, Volume 64, pp. 74-79.

Dylan, Bob. *Bob Dylan Lyrics 1962-1985*, New York: Knoph, 1985.

Encyclopedia of Bible Words, Grand Rapids: Zondervan, 1991.

Hamel, J. *Case Study Method,* Beverly Hills: Sage Publications, 1993.

Holman Bible Dictionary, Nashville: Holman, 1991.

Jowett, Benjamin. *The Dialogues of Plato: Translated by Bejamim Jowett,* Chicago: Encylopedia Britannica, 1952.

Kubler-Ross, Elisabeth. *On Life After Death,* Celestial Arts, 1991.

Lewis, C.S. *Mere Christianity,* San Francisco: Harper, 1952, renewed 1980.

Life Application Study Bible, NIV, Wheaton: Tyndale House Publishers, 1991.

Luthans, F. and T.R.V. Davis. "An Idiographic Approach to Organizational Behavior Research: The Use of Single Case Experimental Designs and Direct Measures," *Academy of Management Review* (7:3), July 1982, pp. 380-391.

Maier, Paul L. *Josephus: The Essential Writings,* Grand Rapids, Kregel Publications, 1988.

McDowell, Josh. *Evidence That Demands A Verdict,* San Bernadino: Here's Life Publishers, 1979

Miller, Madeleine S. and J. Lane Miller. *Harper's Bible Dictionary,* New York: Harper & Row, 1973.

Moody, Raymond A. *Life After Life and Reflections on Life After Life,* New York: Mockingbird Books, 1975.

Moody, Raymond A. *The Light Beyond*, Bantam, 1989.

Moody, Raymond A. *Life After Life: the Investigation of a Phenomenon – Survival After Death*, San Francisco: Harper, 2001.

Ragin, Charles C. and Howard S. Becker. *What is a Case?: Exploring the Foundations of Social Inquiry*, Cambridge: Cambridge University Press, 1992.

Stake, Robert E. *The Art of Case Study Research*, Thousand Oaks, CA: Sage Publications, 1995.

Strobel, Lee. *The Case for Christ: A Journalist's Personal Investigation of the Evidence for Jesus*, Grand Rapids: Zondervan, 1998.

Strobel, Lee. *The Case for Faith*, Grand Rapids: Zondervan, 2000.

The Books of the Bible, Wheaton: Tyndale House Publishers, 1999.

The New Naves Topical Bible, Grand Rapids: Zondervan, 1969.

The NIV Study Bible, Grand Rapids: Zondervan, 1995.

World Book Encyclopedia, Chicago: World Book, 2003.

Yin, R.K. *Case Study Research, Design and Methods*, 3rd Ed. Newbury: Sage Publications, 1994.